DAVID R. ROSS was born with a love of S⟨...⟩
has been fascinated with the history an⟨...⟩ ...ative
soil. This is his sixth book for Luath Press, the first three being
biographies of a trio of Scotland's most famous sons, Wallace,
Bruce and Charles Edward Stuart, and how they have left their
traces on the country's landscape. His fourth book, *A Passion for
Scotland*, was a more general account of Scotland's history, and he
followed that with *Desire Lines*, a tour through the country's history
and landscape on his preferred mode of transport, his beloved
motorcycle.

He is a regular contributor to many magazines, both in
Scotland and for ex-pat Scots abroad. He regularly appears on tel-
evision and radio, often appearing on the History and Discovery
Channels, both here and in North America. The Walk for Wallace
DVD is available from www.scotfilms.com

As the current convener of the Society of William Wallace, Ross
is well known as a public speaker, has been the orator at many
commemorations, and says he is humbled to be able to say a few
words standing on the spots where the great events of Scotland's
story took place. He works tirelessly to promote Scotland, not only
to visitors, but also to the Scots themselves, as he hopes a greater
understanding of her past will make the people of Scotland see the
road ahead into her future; and that road ahead will be one of dignity, and that education will lead to Scotland taking her rightful
place on the world stage.

By the same author:

On the Trail of William Wallace (1999)
On the Trail of Robert the Bruce (1999)
On the Trail of Bonnie Prince Charlie (2000)
A Passion for Scotland (2002)
Desire Lines: A Scottish Odyssey (2004)

David R. Ross

For Freedom

The last days of William Wallace

ANDY HILLHOUSE

DAVID R. ROSS

Luath Press Limited
EDINBURGH

www.luath.co.uk

First published 2005
Reprinted 2006

The paper used in this book is recyclable. It is made from low
chlorine pulps produced in a low energy, low emission manner
from renewable forests.

Printed and bound by
Bell & Bain, Glasgow

Typeset in 10.5 Sabon

Deprive the people of their national consciousness, treat them as a tribe and not a nation, dilute their national pride, do not teach their history, propagate their language as inferior, imply they have a cultural void, emphasise their customs are primitive, and dismiss independence as a barbaric anomaly.

Nazi Reinhard Heydrich
on the Germanisation of Czechoslovakia.

Acknowledgements

Sheila MacLean, for all her hard work keeping the London thing on track; Chris MacLeod for the plaid and her support; Linda Donnelly, for her long hours typing my scrawling into something readable; Kenny Fleming at the Co-op and Hazel Eunson for organising the coffin; all the guys at *Siol nan Gaidheal* for their unquestioning hard work, especially Nick, Finn, Brendan, Jim, Bruce and Scott; Skirlie the Piper; Lynn Boland Richardson for the tickets; *Na Fir Dileas*; James and John Gee; Scott Begbie; Prince Michael of Albany; Sir Tony Paprotny and the rest of the Guarde Ecosse; Doug, David and Christine at the Royal House of Stewart website; Baron Lee, and all the folk of Lanark, especially Margo Steele, Peter Campbell, George Topp, Derek Stewart-Brown and Frank Gunning; the London SNP Members of Parliament and their staff for understanding; all at the Society of William Wallace; Duncan Fenton; Ken Shirra; Andy Hillhouse; Audra McKee and the kids she taught who did all that they could to help; Inspector Hilton and Maxine Worsfold for their diligence in organising the police presence in London; Elspeth King and Michael Donnelly and the staff at the Stirling Smith; Ronnie Browne; Ted Christopher and the members of the Bannockburn Band; *Clann an Drumma*; The Alaska Highlanders; Alex Salmond; Sean Connery; Reverend Alan Sorensen; Fiona Watson; Dr Martin Dudley, Rector of St Bartholomew the Great and all his staff; Christopher Whitton; *Coisir Lunnainn*, the London Gaelic Choir; the staff at the Welsh Centre; Dennis McGhee, my faithful sidekick, and his good lady, Shona; Tim West and Gavin MacDougall and everyone at Luath Press; Rick Wood and the crew at TVP; all the people who donated funds to make it work; my daughter Kimberley for putting up with my Scottish foibles; And last but not least, Sir William Wallace, for doing it all in the first place, going on before and showing us the way.

Contents

Seven Hundred Years

And how did you go to your death?
Did you hold the martyr's defiance that our fathers proudly told,
Or did you scream for mercy at the butcher's cut:
A mortal man on the edge of the abyss?

Where were your thoughts that final day?
Did you drift homewards,
Clinging to the last images of the land you held so dear,
Or did you mind your days of learning and struggle above the noise
To place you soul in the hands of a higher judgement?

And how did the eyes of London see your passing?
Did they hate you as a traitor and a killer of priests and bairns,
Revelling in the justice of your spilling blood?
Surely there were those clutching their own breasts
As the beating heart was torn from your frame,
Dwelling on the thinnest thread that held their earthly life.

Perhaps it was still hatred you clung to.
A rage to dull the pain until the merciful axe fell.
To have met them to their beards –
Had that not been enough for one man and one life time,
Cressingham's bloated corpse consolation for your own?

Or was it Falkirk's Field and failure that haunted your dying thoughts,
In a despair that cried 'All for nought' – the fight is lost!
So courage does not prevail over steel and gold, fear and greed.
Were doubt and terror your only companions at Smithfield?

Can we honour such a man in stone and words alone –
In poetry and film?
A man of deeds and courage lives on in deeds and courage,
Or not at all.
To live meekly by the rule of another shames us all
And shames us still.

Alan Reid
July 2004

CHAPTER ONE

Setting the Scene

IN 2004, I STOOD ON THE TERRACING at Hampden Park in Glasgow, as I had so many times before. I could have sat down on the seat behind me, but I was on my feet applauding the men in the dark blue jerseys of the Scotland football team emerging from the tunnel opposite. They would walk out of the darkness and – as if the sudden exposure to the acclaim of the crowd was a signal – they would break into a jog, one by one, and fan out over the surface of the playing field. There is something almost primeval in the sensation aroused in a football crowd, and in Scotland's case there is once again that sense of gathering, of expectation, that must have been inherent at Stirling Bridge in 1297: camaraderie. A familiarity. One common bond in the crowd. All Scots together, banners flying, chanting familiar slogans and war cries.

John Prebble said of it that: 'the crowd at Hampden roar a terrible truth from their ignorant defiance' – and they do. The Lion of Scotland still stalks its way through that crowd – a little stiff, perhaps, after its years in enforced captivity – but it still has its claws, however long unused.

But the Tartan Army, as the crowd of Scotland supporters calls itself, is comprised only of foot soldiers. There are no leaders, no commanders among their number. They are leaderless, a little like the Scotland they represent, but they know the name of a leader from the past: William Wallace. That is a name that means something to them all. They know that he was just like them, just one of the boys, but he came to the fore when they needed him. Some see Wallace purely and simply as a 'hero', some know his story in depth, some even know of his political manoeuvrings, but his name certainly means something deep inside them all.

What I'm trying to say here, although it hardly needs to be said, is that Wallace is important to Scots, and obviously he is important to me. His status is somehow different from that of heroes in other countries. Wallace holds a place in the psyche that, say, Nelson does not in England, and the idea of Wallace himself is built into the makeup of what constitutes a Scot.

But there are many aspects of history that the Scottish psyche sees differently from its southern counterparts. We Scots commemorate our defeats with a reverence that other nations find baffling. When the Tartan Army message board on the Internet mentioned that commemorations for Wallace were to be held in 2005, one or two of the English posters said, 'This was 700 years ago. What's the point?' But we see the point. It is as if we are confirming who we are and where we have come from. Wallace was one of ours and fought for something we believe in. Seven centuries mean nothing, and there is no cut-off point, no time limit after which his story suddenly does not matter.

Very, very seldom, when I mention holding some sort of Wallace commemoration in Scotland, do any of my country folk say that Wallace now lived so long ago that it does not matter. They just accept it as a part of what Scotland is all about. It is not limited to Wallace, of course, for many other Scots come into this category – Robert the Bruce is another obvious example – but Wallace remains still the hero of the people.

Perhaps this is because the current political situation in Scotland has similarities with Wallace's time. Not the violence of course, but in the fact that we are ruled from somewhere else. The flag of our nation, arguably the oldest national emblem on Earth, does not fly outside the European Parliament or the United Nations. Because of this, Wallace, who fought for the freedom of his people, still matters.

There seems to be an inherent trait in Scots not only to recall our great victories, like Stirling Bridge and Bannockburn, but to remember our defeats too. There is a phenomenon in the Border towns called the Common Ridings, which are held as gala weekends in many of the Scottish Border towns in close proximity to England. The central events in these 'ridings' involve horseflesh, with many riding out en masse to check their town boundaries for any incursions by the English. Each year a youth is chosen to lead his particular townsfolk – a great honour for the chosen person. The Common Ridings are very festive affairs, family occasions where the whole town turns out, and many return home from elsewhere in Scotland and over the planet to reaffirm their identities. But still there is the historic core behind it all. The Border Ridings are connected with the Battle of Flodden, which took place in 1513. (Most Borderers still simply refer to it as 'Flodden'). It was a huge and terrible defeat, with Scots falling in their thousands, and this area of the country supplied the bulk of the victims. The song written to commemorate Flodden, 'The Flowers of the Forest' by Lady Caroline Nairn, can still draw a tear. A Flodden Society exists today, nearly five hundred years later, and to many in Scotland 'Flodden' is much more than just a name and a date to be learned from a dusty history book.

Culloden was fought in 1746 on a moor near Inverness, far north across the country from Flodden, which lies just over the Scottish-English border. Culloden is a name carved into the souls of many Highlanders, not just in Scotland, but across the globe wherever the descendants of those who fought on that fateful day now reside. Culloden was the end of the clan system; it too is more, much more, than just another forgotten battle from a history book. All across Scotland, from the grasses sighing in the winds of the Border Country to the rough tangle of gorse and heather on the edge of the Highlands at Culloden, these and many other battles still mean something and they are embedded deep within our souls.

I have spoken at commemoration ceremonies on both of these fields and looked out at the Scots faces, and I know the blood in their veins is the same that coursed through those who fought there on the day. Although these two examples I have chosen are defeats, they are pertinent today; you can see people walking the paths and visiting the memorials on these sites, deep in thought about what has gone before. Yet I cannot think of a single defeat in England that stirs the souls of Englishmen in the same way. Not that there is anything wrong with that, of course – each nation is welcome to feel how it sees fit about its own past.

And I am happy with the way the Scots have a maudlin sentiment for their low points, as well as with their ability to celebrate their highlights. It is part of who and what we are, and it does not matter if, where Wallace is concerned, I am told: 'But it was 700 years ago!' It still matters to me, and it matters to many other Scots. Wallace died far from home, died among a crowd baying for his torture and death – a death of despair indeed, with not a face to turn to in his final moments of extremity that was not contorted with hatred. I know that even then he thought of Scotland. And that hurts. So I wanted to find some way of showing that, 700 years on, we still care. We know that you have returned to the dust, back to the elements from whence you came, but I also wanted you to know that you are still appreciated, William.

So I have written what is contained within these pages for several reasons. I wanted to commemorate Wallace. I wanted to do a little something, 700 years on, to prove that we remembered the man and that he was not forgotten. I wanted to do something for other Scots, to tell them details of some of the places I have been, walking his last route through London, because nearly everyone can do that if they so desire. So this is a story with several threads, but they are all held together by the name of one man – William Wallace.

When Walter Bower finished writing the *Scotichronicon* – that great chronicle of Scotland – in the 1440s, he wrote 'Christ! He is not a Scot who is not pleased with this book.' I hope that Scots will take something from what I have done or listed here, and it will mean something to them.

On the terraces at Hampden, as the team issued from the tunnel, my mate Brendan, who runs Wallace Day up at Stonehaven – a yearly event with a march through the town that continues on to Dunnottar Castle, with a ceilidh held at night – made a comment at my shoulder. 'Isn't it brilliant being Scottish?' he said. I knew what he meant, as I'm quite happy being Scottish (it's just her subjected status that I don't like) but I knew there must be an underlying reason for his saying it.

'What's your point?' I enquired.

He replied 'It's a hard shift being Scottish, but...'

By 'a hard shift', he was using a term that Scots sometimes use – for example, when one does shift work in the course of one's employment, e.g. from 6:00AM till 2:00PM, 2:00PM till 10:00PM, 10:00PM till 6:00AM and so on, there is always one shift that is seen as being harder than the rest: a hard shift. And it is a hard shift being Scottish, for being a Scot means that you are one of a nation that has done great deeds on a worldwide basis that far outstrip its meagre population on a planetary scale. We have produced scholars and poets famous worldwide; we have invented many of the devices that the planet takes for granted; yet we do not rule ourselves. A hard shift indeed.

'But', he went on, 'there are only five million of us. There are 1,000 million Chinese, 300 million Americans, 250 million Russians, and five million Scots. The chances of being Scottish out of the whole population of the world are infinitesimal. And I'm lucky to be one.'

I'm lucky to be one too. So this is the story of Wallace and of being Scottish, and of how the two are linked.

CHAPTER TWO

The Legacy

WALLACE HAS BEEN THERE through the centuries in Scotland. I'm sure that the way people here and now, in the Scotland of the early twenty-first century, talk of Wallace as a figurehead, with a certain reverence, is not too far removed from the way Wallace was spoken of in, say, the 1600s.

Much of this is due, of course, to the political sway of our southern neighbour England, for that country contains 10 times the population of Scotland, and always has. There are 50 million English to five million Scots today; there were perhaps 500,000 souls in Scotland in Wallace's day to five million English; so the ratios were the same. But it has not just been the preponderance of manpower that has been to England's advantage. England is a far wealthier country than Scotland. More fertile landscape, closer proximity to mainland Europe; it has always been more of a monetary centre too, at least in the London area.

When Scotland has not been annexed to England through political union, there has always been a threat of absorption; it always seems to be the case that the greater eventually erases the lesser. In light of this continued threat, which has not lessened over the centuries, it is not surprising that one individual has been held up as a figurehead for those who wish Scots to have the say over what happens in Scotland. He has been re-invented to suit the circumstances of the last 700 years.

The old, post-Wallace chronicles talk of the man – nay, the giant – who was there for his country in its time of need. In the reign of King James IV of Scotland (1488 – 1513), money was put aside, twenty-six shillings no less (£1.30 in decimal coinage) for the upkeep of Wallace's sword – a venerated object. Blind Harry had already done his round of lordly establishments, relating the deeds of 'Sir William Wallace, the Knight of Elderslie', and when these tales were written down, the result became a best seller. Blind Harry's *Wallace* always has been, in fact – it is the second biggest seller of all time in Scotland, only surpassed by sales of the Bible.

I can see generations of Scottish fathers regaling their sons with tales of Wallace in the glow of the firelight. This certainly happened in the boyhood of Robert Burns, our national bard, as he related how the 'story of Wallace opened a Scottish prejudice in my veins that would boil along till the floodgates of life shut in eternal rest.' Even Napoleon is said to have had a copy of Blind Harry's work at his side on his travels, the martial story of Wallace providing him with inspiration. Burns was so moved by the story of Wallace as written by Harry, he stated that he hoped one day to become a talented enough rhymer to do justice to the man. This came to pass when Burns penned the words to fit an old song called 'Hey Tuttie Tattie', an old marching song from the time of Wallace. (The song is also said to have been familiar to Joan of Arc, the French heroine, as it was played by her *Guarde Ecosse*, or Scots guard, which acted as her bodyguard.)

Burns' lyrics, or 'Scots Wha Hae', ran –

Scots wha hae wi' Wallace bled
Scots wham Bruce has often led
Welcome to your gory bed
Or to victory

Now's the day and now's the hour
See the front of battle lour
See approach proud Edward's power
Chains and slavery

Wha would be a traitor knave?
Wha would fill a coward's grave?
Wha sae base as be a slave?
Let him turn and flee

Wha for Scotland's king and law
Freedom's sword would strongly draw
Freeman stand or freeman fall
Let him on with me

By oppression's woes and pains
By your sons in servile chains
We would drain our dearest veins
But they shall be free

Lay the proud usurper low
Tyrants fall in every foe
Liberty's in every blow
Let us do or die!

Ever since, Burns' piece has been regarded as one of the National Anthems of Scotland. Yet, Scots have at times been jailed for singing it. It sometimes amazes me, the resilience that Scots have, and their ability to remain Scots in the face of great adversity. The Gaelic tongue was outlawed, the tartans that we wear were banned, the clan system destroyed, yet even with a media controlled from England, we still survive.

The biggest problem facing us, however, is the amount of Scots who are indoctrinated by this media and who seem happy to be governed from elsewhere. They see their industries destroyed, their resources stripped, their countryside exploited, and yet still they vote to maintain a government in England capable of doing such things. This I have never been able to understand. Yet there has always been the opposite side of the coin. There have always been Scots who have cherished the ancient freedoms of their nation, who recall the liberties of their forefathers, who understood what their ancestors meant when they signed the Declaration of Arbroath in 1320:

> *For as long as a hundred of us remain alive, we will not*
> *submit to the domination of the English, for it is not*

*glory, honour or riches that we fight for, but for our free-
dom alone, which no one gives up but with life itself.*

Too many people think that being pro-Scottish means being
anti-English. This is merely propaganda. To have a pride in your
own country means nothing more than that. Too often I have seen
friends say that they are pro-Scottish, only to have someone in the
company retort, 'so you hate the English then?' Where does this
come from? The English have been our traditional enemy over the
centuries, but that does not mean that I have any hatred of them. I
only wish my country to be in charge of its own destiny, for better
or worse, and it appals me when people wrap some sort of anti-
English blanket around that standpoint.

Wallace began his campaign because of the invasion perpetrated
by Edward Longshanks, and because of the deprivations being carried out against Scotland and her people. He did not wage war
against the English for the sake of it, or because they were English.
He did it out of necessity, and it makes no difference who the aggressor was. Wallace raised his head when his country lay defenceless.

He may have died terribly, in a way that cannot be outdone in
terms of horror or depravity, but he fought for Scotland and actually defeated England on the battlefield. He also, and this is a very
valid point we should never overlook, acted the diplomat. He sent
letters to foreign traders welcoming them to Scotland; he travelled
to Rome to speak with the Pope, asking for his help in curtailing
English incursions.

He acted, in short, in a pro-Scottish manner. The fact that
Wallace felt justified in travelling to see the Pope, then the most
powerful individual in the Christian world, shows that he did not
think of himself as an aggressor.

Wallace's legacy is extraordinary. He broke the feudal bonds
inherent in his time, and everything that was not to Scotland's
immediate benefit he left by the wayside. He faced up to and over-
rode the lords of his nation who would not come to her aid.

There seems to be a continuing aspect of being Scottish that is
inherent within the psyche of certain individuals from that section

of the population that does not put Scotland first. It was there in Wallace's day: we should never forget that he was betrayed by a Scot. And in more recent times I can recall Michael Forsyth, also a Scot, the English-appointed Secretary of State for Scotland, leaving the premiere of the motion picture *Braveheart* in Stirling and announcing to the media that Wallace was a 'loser'. Wallace did, of course, lose his personal battle against English expansionism. In light of the legacy he has left and the way Scots perceive him, however, and the fact that he is a talisman to his people, it seems rather crude to think of him as a 'loser'. He died in similar circumstances to Jesus Christ, but most would think it a bit off the mark to describe *him* as a loser.

You would expect a politician to be aware of the potency of Wallace as a symbol, even one depicted on the celluloid screen. Although a Scot, Forsyth was in a position of power bestowed by London – again, it shows the relationship between the Scots of Wallace's time and the English with whom they sided against their own, and that side of the aspect has never gone away.

Braveheart was about solidarity, or the lack of it here, and hearing the word 'loser' used in relation to William Wallace made me realise that Mr Forsyth had missed the point completely. *Braveheart* may have its faults, but there is an underlying trend throughout the film that gives an accurate depiction of how some Scots feel and where they think their duty lies. Randall Wallace, its scriptwriter, an American, seems to have hit the nail on the head regarding what Scotland is and what it can be about when he pens lines of script like: 'This country has got no sense of itself. Its nobles share allegiance with England. Its clans war with each other.' And to the 'ruling classes' in that same film, William Wallace says: 'You think the people of this country exist to provide you with position. I think your position exists to provide those people with freedom.'

Wallace, in reality, had to largely ignore the privileged or ruling class in Scotland, who did indeed side with England, because there was gain for them in doing so or because they had been brought up in an environment where it was acceptable to do so. The ordinary folk of Scotland thought differently and, as people do in these circumstances, looked for a leader, whom they found in the shape of Wallace.

It is my experience in modern Scotland that the bulk of those with privilege regard themselves as 'British', again because they believe there is gain in doing so, or because they have been schooled into an environment where this is the accepted norm. Why would any right-thinking individual want their people to be ruled from another country? The ordinary folk of Scotland are the ones who see the country as a nation state, which it is; one that should be in charge of its own destiny. These people see Wallace as their figurehead, one who stood when others would not, and they understand the unselfishness of that stance.

Wallace stands for a particular mindset. We have politicians who try and weigh up the plus and minus points of such a scenario as Scottish independence. England changes the rules regularly. Fishing boundaries are a prime example. And during the referendum of 1979, the boundaries governing the voting procedure were changed, so it was not just the party which had the most votes that won, but a line was set where the winner needed at least 40% of the vote of the whole electorate. As only a small percentage of the population ever bothers to vote, this meant that London was sure the idea of Scottish autonomy was going to be kept an unreachable dream.

I often wonder what a politician of the calibre of Wallace would have made of it if he were alive today. Would he have stood by and happily taken whatever judgement was meted out to his own from elsewhere? I doubt it. This is much of what makes Wallace so pertinent to the people of Scotland today. It is the longing for a figurehead who will cut through the pontificating and procrastination, to say 'no more!' where Scotland is concerned.

Each generation recognises Wallace as a symbol of their freedom. And so for seven centuries this ordinary man of flesh and blood has become a totem in the extraordinary mindset of longing in the Scots, who hang his memory up as a symbol of what we can be. What we could be. Wallace has this legacy, a legacy that very few in history can attain, no matter how much of it is imagination or wishful thinking. Is he really a loser?

CHAPTER THREE

From Capture to London

BLIND HARRY TELLS US THAT Sir John Stewart of Menteith agreed to betray Wallace to the English in the church at Rutherglen.

> *Edward he sends for Aymer de Vallance now,*
> *And asks at him what he thought best to do*
> *Who like a traitor, answered and said,*
> *'Doubtless he by some friend must be betrayed*
> *Or by some of his good companions sold*
> *Who have the best liking to the English Gold'*
> *Thus Vallance does the treason undertake,*
> *To Scotland comes, at Bothwell did arrive,*
> *To execute the plot he did contrive*
> *Unto Sir John Menteith express did send*
> *To come and speak with him at Rutherglen.*

In the church, Menteith informs the English of his price for delivering Wallace. There are scant remains of this church still standing. They are in the graveyard on Rutherglen's Main Street, just to the west of the Town Hall, a noticeable landmark with a tall tower visible for miles around. It is unfortunate that this tower flies a very visible Union Jack, or perhaps it is fitting, as the church – where the dastardliest deed of betrayal in the history of Scotland took place – sits in the shadow of this flapping symbol.

All that remains of the church is a gable wall, to which has been attached a slightly later bell tower, but as you walk round to where the body of the building originally stood, you are where the 'False' Menteith decided to become one of the most hated men in the history of Scotland: the betrayer of Wallace.

Blind Harry tells us that Wallace was godfather to two of

Menteith's children. We have no way of knowing if this is true, but the one thing that seems obvious is that Wallace trusted Menteith. The English must have been delighted at this confidante of Wallace agreeing to help them in exchange for money and title. So who then was Menteith?

The name 'Menteith' comes from the high ground to the north of the Lake of Menteith, near Callander in Perthshire. The high ground separating river systems in Scotland is known as a 'mounth', so the title is a corruption of the Mounth of the Teith, the Teith being the name of a fast-flowing river that flows east to join the River Forth just before Stirling.

The first Earl of Menteith was Gilchrist, who appears in our records in the time of Malcolm IV (1153 – 1165). The earldom passed to the Comyn family, and when Walter Comyn died in 1258 he was one of the Regents of Scotland in the minority of Alexander III. It then passed to his brother-in-law, Walter Steward, the third son of the third High Steward of Scotland. Sir John Stewart, the betrayer, was his son. He had originally been a strong supporter of the Scottish cause, but when Longshanks began to gain the upper hand in wresting control of Scotland, Menteith, along with many others, came into Longshanks' 'peace'. It is probable that, in his case, this occurred in the winter of 1303-1304. Menteith was rewarded for this defection to the English cause by being appointed Sheriff of Dumbarton and keeper of its castle. I am constantly amazed at how people can turn their back on their own nation and take the side of another for position and wealth. His original family home stood on the island of Inch Tulla in the Lake of Menteith, only scant ruins of which now remain. It is sometimes said that the Lake of Menteith is called 'lake' rather than 'loch' because of its associations with the False Menteith, but this anomaly is actually due to a cartographer's mistake and the name has stuck. I think we should all refer to it as the Loch of Menteith again to get the name back to its original usage!

Longshanks made it clear that he was keeping a close eye on those Scots who submitted to him. In one document Longshanks declares 'Sir Simon Frazer (sic), Sir John Comyn, Sir Alexander Lindsay and Sir David Graham, are to exert themselves until twenty days after Christmas to capture William Wallace and hand him over to the King. And the King will take careful note of how each conducts himself, so that he may show most favour to the one who takes him with regard to mitigation of his sentence of exile or fine.' Edward Longshanks also told them that any personal penalties that were being held against them for taking the side of Scotland would be 'eased' when Wallace was captured. How hard any of these Scots tried to actually capture Wallace is anyone's conjecture. Sir Simon Fraser had until very recently been a companion-in-arms of Wallace, and after Wallace's death joined King Robert the Bruce's campaign. He was eventually captured, though, and his head joined that of Wallace on London Bridge. So it would seem that many of Wallace's former comrades simply made the right noises, making it look as if they were hot on Wallace's trail, but other nobles would have been in a position of real and extreme dislike of Wallace. They had seen him strip their powers and would have regarded him as an upstart against their lineage and nobility; they would even have been jealous of Wallace's position as the people's champion. But all this is of no matter, as Menteith was the man who did the deed.

The story of Wallace's betrayal runs along these lines:

Edward Longshanks had settled in to besiege Stirling Castle, and it had held out under extreme conditions under the guidance of its keeper, Sir William Oliphant. When it fell in July 1304, one of the garrison, Ralph de Haliburton, was taken south for imprisonment in England. It is believed that Wallace would have been familiar with this individual, as members of Haliburton's family had fought with Wallace earlier in his career.

On 28 February 1305 Haliburton was released from English captivity on the condition that he helped to capture Wallace. This is reported in the English chronicle of Peter of Langtoft. Haliburton became the responsibility of yet another Scottish knight who had submitted to Edward of England, Sir John Mowbray. But Haliburton seemed to drift into the company of Menteith. We can only assume that he worked for Menteith in the role of double agent, managing to ingratiate himself with Wallace in some way, but reporting what he could glean back to Menteith at Dumbarton. It would seem that Haliburton managed to join Wallace's small company.

Near the end of Wallace's career, the English hold on Scotland was particularly strong. His companions were dependent on one another, and were what would have been referred to in the American Wild West as 'desperate men'. English gold was flowing in evidence, buying traitorous Scots or information, and there was an ever-tightening noose around the few remaining pockets of Scottish resistance. Wallace's men had seen much action and were probably at the stage of using cold steel first and asking questions later. There had already been several narrow escapes from English capture. Wallace and Sir Simon Fraser had had a furious fight to escape a force of the enemy at Happrew near Peebles, where they managed to cut their way out of a surprise attack. (The place name still survives in local farms, such as Easter Happrew.)

An even more frenzied affair took place at Black Earnside in September 1304. There has been much debate as to when this fight took place, due to its being placed at various stages in Wallace's career by Blind Harry and other chroniclers, but there is no reason to suppose the English chronicles are incorrect. This battle, according to local tradition, was fought on the hillside above Lindores Abbey, near Newburgh on the Firth of Tay. Aymer de Valence, who was one of King Edward's most able soldiers and had been created Earl of Pembroke, led the English in this fight. He was born in 1270, so was of an age with Wallace. He fought against Bruce at Loudoun Hill and Bannockburn, both of which were English defeats, although he defeated Bruce early in his career at Methven. He died in 1324, and is buried in Westminster Abbey opposite the tomb of Longshanks himself. His father was a half-brother of Longshanks, so they would have been able to call each other 'cousin'. De Valence rode in under the Flag of St George and had 300 archers in his company. Probably only the most battle-hardened of Wallace's company survived, so if Haliburton had indeed been allowed to join this band, there must have been a fair degree of trust involved. It seems that Wallace had no reason to distrust either Menteith or Haliburton.

Wallace was captured at Robroyston, near Bishopbriggs, in the Glasgow area around midnight on 3 August 1305. The legends surrounding his capture say that once Wallace and his companions were asleep, Haliburton stole away to inform Menteith, and the barn in which they slept was quickly surrounded. But why was Wallace in the Glasgow area?

Blind Harry says that he was there to meet secretly with Robert the Bruce – a distant possibility. It is also possible that he was trying to make contact with Robert Wishart, the Bishop of Glasgow. The land thereabouts belonged to Glasgow Cathedral, hence the name Bishopbriggs, which is a modern corruption of the 'bishop's riggs', (riggs being a Scots term for fields). Wishart was always a strong supporter of the struggle for Scottish independence, and the cathedral is only a few miles distant. This was open countryside until only a few years ago, and it seems there was quite a bit of woodland in this area in the early 1300s.

The name Robroyston seems to cause confusion too. I have often been asked if there is any connection with Rob Roy McGregor, another famous Scot, albeit one who lived a few centuries after Wallace. There is an abiding story that it is named after one Ralph Raa, who helped to betray Wallace, but this may be no more than legend. The *Ordnance Gazetteer of Scotland*, published in 1893, has this entry – 'an estate, with a modern mansion, in Cadder parish, Lanarkshire, 4 miles NE of Glasgow. A cottage on it, standing till 1826, is said to have been the place where Sir William Wallace was betrayed to the English. A neighbouring lake, which figures in the story of the patriot's betrayal, has been nearly all drained, and is now represented by a gloomy expanse, partially engirt with pine trees.'

When this cottage or barn – depending on which source you read – was demolished, Sir Walter Scott managed to glean some of the wood (the rafters I believe) and had furniture created from it. I remember one of the chairs on display at the Stirling Smith Art

Gallery and Museum on the 700th anniversary of the battle of Stirling Bridge in 1997. I had a wee sit in it when no one was looking, but please don't tell anybody!

I somehow feel that even if Wallace was destined to meet with Bruce, Wishart figures somewhere in this equation, for the situation at the time was pretty desperate. Most of Scotland was under the English heel, and not only the English were hunting Wallace down. Many Scots were after him too, determined to gain English Edward's favour. Wishart had always helped the Scottish cause, and Wallace would have needed money, perhaps food, perhaps just some comfort from a man of God to bolster him in his time of need. I don't for a minute believe that Wallace felt he was taking the wrong road where Scotland was concerned. Even if every other man in Scotland bent the knee to England, Wallace would have had none of it. His country was in the hands of an alien race. Wallace would not have cared if the whole world thought him wrong; he knew that a country controlled from elsewhere is a hateful thing. If he had given up on Scotland, he would have given up on everything he believed in, and he would no longer have been William Wallace. So he stuck to his principles, because he was a Scot and a patriot. He could never have known that his stance in those last few months of his life would make such a huge difference to the future of his country.

He could have disappeared, fled abroad perhaps, to sell his sword as a mercenary in some European conflict, or even just to have some peace and live a quiet life. But he was true to the end, true to himself and his country, and Scotland has loved him for it ever since, every generation that cherishes freedom having embraced his memory.

As Wallace spent his last free moments on the land of Glasgow Cathedral, we should perhaps talk a little of the cathedral itself. I suppose most Scots, and Glaswegians too for that matter, don't really realise that Glasgow has the best-preserved early cathedral in Scotland. The building was consecrated in 1160 and has been in use ever since. The populace of the city protected their cathedral during the turbulent days of the Reformation. Wishart himself is buried at the back of the crypt, but you may have a little trouble locating the tomb of this patriot freedom fighter who did so much for his country. He presided over Bruce's coronation and was chained in an English prison for his trouble, and although Bruce managed to ransom prisoners from Bannockburn to gain his release, Wishart would never see his beloved Scotland again. He went blind during his harsh imprisonment, but at least breathed the air of a Scotland rid of the invader during his final days. His is the defaced tomb, on the left side of the little chapel at the far right hand side at the rear of the crypt; the head is missing, and Union Flags hang above his last resting place. There are rows of steps just before the place where Wishart lies. Wallace would have sat here at times, waiting near the back of the cathedral where the Molendinar once ran, the little stream where Glasgow was founded, now tunnelled in out of sight. St Mungo, the patron saint of Glasgow and for that matter the first Glaswegian, the founder of the city, is also buried down here in the crypt, and in his own day Wallace must have viewed his tomb.

On the night of his capture, Wallace was rudely awakened by English soldiers and Scots traitors piling into the barn. One English chronicler, Peter of Langtoft, reported that Wallace was asleep beside his mistress, but Blind Harry reports that he was with one of his most loyal followers, Kerlie, who was cut down on the spot. Kerlie came from Cruggleton on the Solway coast, where today stand the ruins of Cruggleton Castle, his family's property.

It seems that Menteith was the overseer at Wallace's actual capture. Blind Harry reports a strange tale in which Menteith says that Wallace must not resist, and if he is willing to lay down his weapons and be tied, Menteith will try to smuggle him past the waiting English soldiers. Whether this is true or not we have no way of knowing, but it again implies that Wallace trusted Menteith. But trust or not, Wallace was taken. I can imagine him glancing left and right, looking for a way to escape. Perhaps he was beaten to render him insensible. His captors went through his pockets and found several documents on his person, although what information these documents held is mostly unknown. It is said there was correspondence between Wallace and some of the leading magnates of Scotland, and I suppose it is possible that one of these documents would explain why he was in the Glasgow area, as it may have contained the details of an appointment. It is doubtful there were letters that incriminated other Scots taken from Wallace on his capture, as there do not appear anywhere on the records details of arrests elsewhere immediately afterwards as you would have expected had documents such as these been on his person.

Only one letter has survived; the rest of Wallace's papers have disappeared over the centuries. The surviving letter was one of recommendation, given to Wallace by King Philip IV of France for Wallace to present to the French officials at the Vatican. It stems from Wallace's journey abroad, when he acted the diplomat on Scotland's behalf, visiting France and then Rome to try and bring pressure to bear against Edward and England. It is dated 7 November 1300, and is worded as follows, translated from the French of the original:

Philip K. of France to his lieges at the Roman Court. Commands them to request the Pope's favour for his beloved William le Walies of Scotland knight, in the matters which he wishes to forward with His Holiness. Monday after All Saints. Pierrefonds.

(I give here a slightly different translation than that used in my book *On the Trail of William Wallace*, as they vary from source to source.)

This letter is so very important to the history of Scotland: it is the only item that survives which we know was a personal possession of Wallace. It was in his pocket or pouch when he was taken; it is something he held and looked upon, and we too can look upon it today.

Another letter, known as the Lübeck letter, which bears Wallace's seal, may have been written and sealed by scribes, although Wallace may have read it and applied his own seal, but we do not and never will know for sure. There has also been some doubt cast over the origins of the famous Wallace Sword kept at the National Wallace Monument on the Abbey Craig, although I think there is enough evidence to link it with William. The Lübeck letter is kept in the museum of the town of that name, near Hamburg in Germany, which is understandable as that particular letter was sent there after the Battle of Stirling Bridge. But the letter of safe conduct from the King of France was a personal possession of Wallace, and the only one we have. It is kept in the Public Records Office at Kew in England, along with the actual ledger into which the scribe recorded the details of Wallace's 'trial'. All three items were on loan for a short period to the Museum of Scotland in Chambers Street in Edinburgh. Everyone around me was looking at the Lübeck letter, as it had made newspaper headlines when it was 'rediscovered' in the late 1990s, but I looked at that wee letter from France – and it is wee, a few inches across and only an inch or two in depth, with a seal attached. I knew it had been taken from Wallace and sent south accompanying him on his final journey, so it really meant something to me to see it. Something Wallace had owned that I could look at too – suddenly there was a little bond between us across the seven centuries.

Why is this letter not on show in Scotland? It is a Scottish document, taken from a Scot in Scotland, and it should be there for the people of this country to look at whenever they want. In fact, the more I go looking for documents, the more I find that the ones particularly relevant to Scotland are kept in England and are never on show to the general public. Everything I have ever hunted for pertaining to the Bruce family is held down south. Even a rare treasure like the Prayer Book of St Margaret of Scotland, queen of Malcolm Canmore, is kept in the Bodleian Library at Oxford. Why is this? Why are museums and archives in Scotland not demanding these items of our history back at once? It is the shadow of unionism I'm afraid. When freedom comes, these documents and artefacts should be returned.

The site of the house or barn where Wallace was captured is today marked by a large Celtic cross, adorned with a two handed sword, atop a cairn. This monument stands in Wallace Well Road, so called because a little beyond the monument there is an old well, called – not surprisingly – the Wallace Well. The well has been land-scaped and walled in, but could do with constant repair work. I am often asked what the connection to Wallace is, and generally tell people that because of its proximity to the capture site, it is possible Wallace had his last drink as a free man here. It has been known as the Wallace Well for centuries, but the real connection is lost in the mists of time. It has lost its preservation listing by Historic Scotland, which is a shame as it is now more at risk from developers. We have so little that is tangible connected to our national hero that these sites should be cherished.

The monument at the house site itself was raised by public subscription, the fund of which was begun by the Reverend David MacRae of the Scottish Patriotic Society, and was unveiled at a ceremony in 1900. The Clan Wallace Society of North America paid for restoration work in 1986, and a granite block with a plaque telling the story was sited just in front of the monument within the surrounding railings, although this wee addition was stolen in 1996. I suppose I can understand someone wanting to take something with a Wallace connection, however tenuous, but a granite block from the Wallace Society of North America? Bloody heavy too, I would imagine, getting it over the surrounding railings. The Society of William Wallace has placed a new plaque on the site of the North American one. It was put in place in August 2000 to mark the 100th anniversary of the monument. The monument has the story of Wallace's capture on the front, inscriptions on the side, and Roman numerals stating '1305' on the shaft. The inscription on front of the monument states: 'This monument, raised in 1900 by public subscription, marks the site of the house in which the hero of Scotland was basely betrayed around midnight on 5 August 1305, along with his compatriot Kerlie, who was slain.' Now, this is a bit strange, because the English accounts state that Wallace was taken on 3 August, and I have no idea why it says 5 August on the monument, but it does. Please don't let this slip detract from the solemnity of the spot.

This location has changed hugely over the last decade or so. As you can see from the old description in the *Ordnance Gazetteer of Scotland*, there used to be a small loch in this area, and a large house once stood about 50 metres behind the spot where the monument now stands. In 2002 an archaeological exploration actually uncovered the outline of this house, but it has no real Wallace connection other than its location. In the mid 1990s this was an area surrounded by fields and hedgerows, with a view out to Ben Lomond on a clear day. New housing developments grow ever closer, however, and in 2005 they are within sight of the monument and many of the fields have been swallowed up.

Just a few years ago, there was a block of two semi-detached modern houses just to the right of the monument, and Robroyston Mains farm was almost adjacent across the road. The houses have gone and only vestiges remain of the farm, which is a shame. The walls of the farm were created from rubble, not dressed stone, which shows it must have been of considerable antiquity. I remember going for a walk through its rooms when it first became derelict. It was an interesting old place, and it is a shame that the foresight or the will was not in place to have at least saved the main building as a visitor centre. There is actually nowhere to park near the monument, and it is a case of just pulling over in a car and leaving your hazard warning lights on – not the best option, but the only one available. It is the old story: if you build it, they will come. A wee information centre with a few story boards and some parking spaces available would have had people visit, right on the edge of Glasgow as this site is.

I have several times said a few words at the commemoration ceremony held here every year on the nearest Saturday to 3 August, and the people attending must always keep out of the way of oncoming traffic and struggle to hear the speeches above the noise. The site looks very run down too, and I feel that this is a place of such importance that it should be a priority to keep it looking its best. Members of the Society of William Wallace have painted the fence, and one member even turns up to cut the grass on occasion, because Wallace still means something in some quarters in

Scotland. One thing that made me feel a bit better was that on one personal visit a Glasgow City Council pick up truck pulled up; its occupants told me that they often drove by 'just to have a look and keep an eye on the place.' It was obvious that they did this because they cared and not because it was officially a duty.

If you wish to find this memorial, I will do my best with directions, but because there is constant building work going on in the vicinity these may change, although you will be able to discover the general area. If you are on the M8 eastbound through Glasgow, you will see the turn off for Stirling a little after Glasgow Cathedral. This is the M80. The first turn off on this road is marked 'Bishopbriggs, B765'. At the roundabout below the M80 Stirling Road, which you have just exited, turn left. There is a large Asda supermarket here. At the roundabout which gives access to the Asda, take the road signposted Kirkintilloch B765. Driving by the side of the Asda, you are going up a slight gradient and there is another roundabout at the top. All these roundabouts are only a couple of hundred yards apart. At this one you go straight through; the road is marked 'Lenzie B812'. You go downhill to yet another roundabout, and you will be glad to know this is the last. Here you turn right on the exit marked 'Kirkintilloch and Lenzie B812'. The monument is roughly 300 yards down this road on your right. The Wallace Well is several hundred yards further on at a junction.

On a visit in January 2005, I was disgusted at the state of the place. Rubbish everywhere, most of it fly-tipping – bin bags, three-piece suites, even a television lying in the vicinity. I can't believe that Glasgow City Council let this place go to wrack and ruin, but even worse are the scum who think it is a good place to dump rubbish in the first place. It makes you want to weep.

As soon as he was captured, Wallace was shackled and legend states that he was taken to Dumbarton Castle. This is eminently possible of course, as you would expect Menteith to take him to the castle that he was in charge of. If not immediately to Dumbarton, where else would he go? There does not seem to be any other obvious choice, and if Wallace was tied to a horse, as would most likely be the case, Dumbarton was reachable in a few hours. Menteith would have immediately sent out a rider to inform the English hierarchy that Wallace had been taken.

There is not much of any real antiquity on show at Dumbarton Castle today, but it is impressive nonetheless due to its situation at the mouth of the Clyde, and the impressive vistas that unfold as you climb toward the twin peaks of the rock on which the castle stands. If you have never seen Dumbarton Rock, it is a very striking lump of stone to say the least, standing at the end of a peninsula on the left side of the River Leven as it enters the River Clyde. (The River Leven flows south from Loch Lomond.) It is 200 feet high, and is formed of basalt, like Stirling Castle rock, Ailsa Craig, and the Bass Rock, but unlike Stirling Castle rock, there is no sloping, easy side of ascent, and from most angles Dumbarton Rock seems to actually overhang your vantage point. It is a glaringly obvious defensive site, commanding the two rivers, and offering extensive views as well as its natural fortress-like qualities. Early settlers would not have been slow in using it as a place of defence, and certainly the history of the place goes back to hoary antiquity. It has been identified with the Roman naval station 'Theodosia'; in Ossian's story it was 'Balclutha' – the town on the Clyde – and 'Urbs Legionis' – the city of the legion, the scene of Arthur's ninth battle at the beginning of the sixth century. The Arthur connection is interesting, as Arthur was, of course, Arthur of the Britons, and the name Dumbarton means 'fort of the Britons'. In a record from 1367, in the time of King David II, the castle is referred to as 'Castle Arthuri'.

To reach the highest points of Dumbarton Rock, you ascend steps through various defensive works. Above the doorway of one, a contorted face is pointed out as a representation of the 'False Menteith', the betrayer of Wallace. The western summit of the rock is known as 'Wallace's Seat'. Nearby is a ruined building, obviously of two differing ages; the lower courses grey stone, the upper, more modern reddish sandstone, but there is a little plaque that announces that this is 'Wallace's Prison'. Whether the lower courses of stone are part of the building where Wallace was kept, we will probably never know, but tradition obviously points to this spot.

From the summit of the Rock you are in no doubt about the strategic importance of this place. Strangely, from Wallace's Prison you can see up the River Leven to Mains of Cardross, where Robert the Bruce breathed his last in 1329, in a manor he had built for his later years. Wallace, chained and shackled, would not know that just 24 years later Bruce would die with Scotland a free and independent nation state, within sight of this place where he must have despaired for his country's future.

It was probably here at Dumbarton that he discovered he was to be taken south to London, and he would have known that execution was to be his lot, though he would not be sure what method would be used to end his life. The gallows? Beheading? Many times he must have imagined his life ending in battle; a sword thrust and it would be over. Perhaps he expected an assassin's knife, Scotland being again under a predominately English sway. He probably did not foresee the long road that leads south through England being his final journey.

The large two-handed weapon known as the Wallace Sword was displayed at Dumbarton Castle for many centuries. The story is that when Wallace was captured his possessions were carried with him to Dumbarton, and when his journey south began his sword was left behind. It was transferred to the National Wallace Monument atop the Abbey Craig near Stirling in 1888, where it can be seen to this day. Is it really the sword wielded by Wallace? I'm sure he used many weapons in his time, but this is the one reputed to have been with him on the night of his capture. Historians have argued that some of the fittings look more like those on swords from the late 1400s or early 1500s, but this can be explained. On the 200th anniversary of Wallace's murder, 1505, King James iv ordered that the sword 'be bound with cordle of silk, a new hilt and plomet [pommel – the counterweight at the top of the hilt], new scabbard, and a new belt to the said sword – 26 shillings.' One historian has commented that it may be the 'ghost of Wallace's sword', which is fair enough. No matter what, it means something to many Scots. It has been stolen twice, in 1936 and 1972, both times to make a statement regarding the political status of Scotland, and both times it has been returned after a few months. I know a man who was involved in the 1972 incident, which took place when I was still at school, and I can remember my mother telling me the story of the earlier 'disappearance' and how the sword had been 're-discovered' at Bothwell Bridge in Lanarkshire.

Glaswegians travelling 'doon the watter' i.e. down the River Clyde in the summer months on steamships in the 1800s, were entertained by on-deck bands. They would break into a quick burst of 'Scots Wha Hae' as they steamed past the Rock, in tribute to the memory of Wallace. This tradition unfortunately came to an end when the sword was transferred from Dumbarton to the National Wallace Monument in 1888. But back to the story...

The next step was to get Wallace south and into England as soon as possible. We do not have any details of how Wallace was taken south, but his being tied to a horse seems logical. We do not know the route taken either, other than the fact that he passed through Carlisle. Menteith, I would imagine, would have used quiet back roads to ensure against any possible rescue attempts, although as Wallace had, according to legend, only one companion with him at his capture, and as this companion, Kerlie, was slain, it is doubtful if anyone really knew that Wallace had been taken.

With Menteith wanting to have Wallace handed over to English control as soon as possible, it is probable that he was only kept that one night at Dumbarton. We are told that 'divers routes' took him to the Borders, keeping away from well-worn trails. It is possible Wallace was taken across the Clyde in a rowing boat before horses were used to transport him, as there is a Wallace legend connected with the south bank of the Clyde. In the grounds of the Holy Family Presbytery in Parkhill Avenue in Port Glasgow, an ancient oak tree stood until 1995. This tree, as long as records went back, had a chain around it, and it was said that Wallace had been chained to it while his captors stopped for lunch! Perhaps they waited there for fresh horses. When the tree eventually fell, the chain around it was taken by one of the priests from the presbytery and kept as a memento. It was not the original chain, of course, for every time one rusted away it was replaced by another. The last of the line of which I speak is said to have been put in place in the 1800s. Every effort had been made to save the tree as it approached the end of its life, with props being put in place to try and keep it upright for as long as possible. All these little stories are part of the picture of Wallace, and how his memory is perceived by the Scots of today.

Wallace was associated with trees in many parts of Scotland, and it shows how the folk memory of the man has embedded itself into people and places. There was the famous Wallace Oak in the Torwood. Another Wallace Oak once stood at Kirkfieldbank in Clydesdale, and his birthplace, Elderslie, had not only its own Wallace Oak but also a Wallace Yew at the site of his house. I am writing this particular passage in late January 2005, and sadly most of that Wallace Yew fell in a storm on the eleventh of this month. Many trees fell that night, but it seems somehow ironic that this tree happened to fall on the 700th anniversary of his murder. All is being done to save the tree; specialists have been called in to do whatever work is needed to maintain what is left of the yew. I hope that future generations can get to see it still, and that it can survive the extensive damage. (It is reckoned to be only 300 or so years old, yet records from the 1600s refer to 'that ancient tree', so it may be an offspring of the original.)

Trees, rocks, hills and wells: generations of Scots have pointed these places out to their children, telling them how Wallace was once there, how he hid there, how he drank there, how he waylaid Englishmen even though he was sorely outnumbered. It is an astonishing legacy, the people's way of celebrating how an individual stood up for their – and Scotland's – freedom and paid the ultimate price. The countryside of Scotland is covered in such places.

Wallace was taken to Carlisle, his captors most likely going by moorland tracks and keeping away from river valleys, which contained the usual routes, like the one that used the Clyde, then crossed to the Annan or the Nith, which would then lead to the Border. He was probably already in England before word really started to spread that 'Wallace had been taken!' I am often asked why there was no rescue attempt. The speed of it all was probably the cause, plus, even if a handful of patriotic Scots knew what was happening, I'm sure many men-at-arms closely guarded Wallace, thus an attack would have been suicidal.

At Carlisle Wallace was handed over to Sir John Segrave, who was to be Wallace's close companion up to, and after, his death. It was Segrave's responsibility to get him to London without mishap. I'm sure Segrave, hardened soldier though he was, would not have relished having to explain to Edward Longshanks if Wallace had escaped. Wallace and Segrave had crossed paths before. Segrave had been at the battle of Roslin, fought on 24 February 1303. It was around this time that Wallace returned from his trip to Europe, and he may have been present at this battle, in which Segrave was wounded. Roslin was a strange affair, in which three separate English brigades were set upon one by one by a body of Scottish horsemen. Segrave was captured, but an English counter-attack freed him. Roslin was one of those melées where no one was sure of victory, but it showed that the English were not invincible. There is a modern memorial to this battle in Roslin by the rear of the Roslin Institute, in the form of a cairn surrounded by circular wall, which was unveiled on 6 October 1994.

If Wallace was not present at Roslin, he and Segrave certainly met later, in one of Wallace's last recorded encounters with English soldiery. Segrave defeated Wallace – who had a force which included Sir Simon Fraser – in a surprise attack at Happrew, west of Peebles, in 1304. By the time of Happrew, with most of Scotland under Edward Longshanks' sway, to escape with his life against overwhelming odds was probably as much as Wallace could hope for. Yet he continued the struggle. This is one of the reasons he has never been forgotten in Scotland. He continued the struggle, to the very end. Wallace would probably be very proud to know that his name is still a symbol seven centuries on. And his struggle goes on.

From Carlisle south, we have no idea of the actual route. There was no lagging though, as we know Wallace was captured on 3 August and appeared in London on 22 August. Nineteen days may seem quite a lot, but were there any roads to speak of? Unless old Roman roads were used here and there, the journey must have been made on rough and alternately muddy and stony tracks.

It is possible Wallace was taken by an eastern, coastal route. So many English armies of invasion would muster at Newcastle, then cross the Border at Berwick-upon-Tweed to devastate Lothian en route for the central belt of Scotland. I have to at least admit that Wallace may have been taken the 60 or so miles over to Newcastle, to then be taken south by the more level east coast route to London. But time scale makes me think that they must have headed due south from Carlisle, that extra mileage eastwards being a bit too much.

We can only guess at the actual route, whether the line of the modern A6 would have been used, located as it is, of course, on the line of ancient pathways running from town to town. Or, like later armies invading from Scotland in the glory years of Robert the Bruce, perhaps he was taken by the route that follows the River Eden to its source in the Pennine Hills, crossing over into the valley of the River Ure and into Yorkshire before heading south for London. It is a pity that there is no record of where Wallace's party rested each night, but, of course, his captors would see no need of recording such details; they were following Edward of England's orders to get him to London as soon as possible. And Wallace was expected on the twenty-second of August, as the court operations for his sham trial were already in place for the twenty-third.

Wallace was not familiar with England, other than what he had seen on his invasion of the north of that country, where its landscape does not differ greatly from Scotland – although parts of the English north are actually comprised of rougher country and it is more desolate in places than the northern side of the Border. Although he would have been anything but comfortable, and was probably abused and pelted with all types of filth by English folk in every sizeable habitation he passed through (as I am sure the populace was warned of his approach beforehand), I'm sure he was still looking hard at the deep underbelly of the country that had been Scotland's enemy for so long. He must have started to realise that he was to be used as an object of humiliation in London, and he would be trying to school himself to remain emotionless, as much as possible, in the face of this growing apprehension. Wallace was not a stupid man. For that age, he was well travelled and was educated in many of the ways of the world apart from the violent warfare that he was forced to take part in to liberate his people. He would have been battling within to try and come to terms with the unknown that lay ahead. I do know that he knew he was getting further from Scotland by the day, and this must have disheartened him. The chance to escape never came, of course. Blind Harry speaks of the fact that he was 'secured with iron chains that were both stark and keen', but Wallace must have looked at every opportunity and looked back over his shoulder towards the north, towards Scotland, assessing the distance, assessing the route. But he was never to see Scotland again, and he had no idea that the people there were in future to regard him as their national hero.

CHAPTER FOUR

Trial

WALLACE MUST HAVE WATCHED the change in the landscape as he crossed into the flat countryside of south east England, so much more fertile than most of Scotland, and more heavily populated. Although the skyline of London starting to appear before him would have had him filling with apprehension, he must have been quite impressed with the wealth on show, compared to what he was used to in Scotland. The well-dressed and well-fed burgesses, the people and property untouched by war, would have been in contrast to a Scotland being trampled under the feet of a hostile army of occupation. The city walls, stretching out in either direction, were perhaps similar to those he had seen on his travels through Europe. Already the people were beginning to gather, displaying rank hostility towards this brave warrior. Then it was through one of the gates and into the city itself.

A rider had obviously gone ahead to London with the news of Wallace's capture. Edward Longshanks had seen the opportunities in Wallace's apprehension; his chance to show England's might and the righteousness of his campaign to subjugate Scotland. Wallace had defied England, he had defeated an English army at Stirling Bridge eight years before, and now the people would see what happened to anyone who thought they could stand against the power of England's King. Propaganda played its part. All of London – not just the people of the city, but those of the surrounding districts as well – knew that Wallace was coming. The streets were packed, everyone eager to catch a glimpse of the Scottish 'monster'. Tens of thousands of eyes looked upon the man William Wallace. And what he made of it, God only knows. How was the news spread? Perhaps by town criers or the like. Maybe there were men briefed to go out and fire up the passions of the populace – a 'rent-a-mob' situation. I can see a scenario where a speaker would stand up in a market place and shout to those who gathered there that Wallace was coming to the city in chains. This demon who had forced English nuns to dance naked before he butchered them; they, the ordinary people, could actually come and look upon him and see him suffer threefold death.

It seems it was a struggle to make way through the pressing crowds. Armed guards, no matter how much they pushed and shoved and offered threats, seem to have made little impact. People were there in many thousands, the ones at the rear pushing in to try and get a view, and the guards at the very centre of the maelstrom had little chance of making headway. How Wallace was taken through the streets on his entry to the city is open to conjecture. He was probably chained or tied on a horse, surrounded by guards, but he may have been transferred onto a cart of sorts, perhaps similar to the one at the denouement of *Braveheart*, to create a spectacle that we would call in modern parlance a 'photo opportunity'. I'm sure the London mob pelted Wallace with whatever was to hand. I often wonder if he was scared, if he showed fear, or managed to withstand the humilation with head held high. He would know by now that he was to suffer some sort of horrific death, the populace leaving him in no doubt of that, and would have done his best to hold on to dignity, as nothing was going to change the outcome. We know that he managed to shout down his judges in the courtroom, so I'm sure that he rose above the abuse and missiles of the crowd. Wallace had fought tirelessly for Scotland and her people; he was not going to buckle now and allow the righteousness of his struggle for Scottish freedom to be demeaned.

It seems that his destination was the Tower of London, where he was to be incarcerated for the night. I have seen inventories of prisoners of the Tower, and Wallace's name is listed. But Wallace was never within the Tower of London. The press of the crowd was so great that the procession came to a halt. Wallace was taken to the property of one William de Leyre, an alderman of London, who was once a legal sheriff. His house was in the parish of Fenchurch, and Wallace was probably locked – chained – in a cellar or some other secure room. Unfortunately we do not know the exact site of this house, although Fenchurch Street marks the vicinity. It is interesting to look at a map of old London, the old medieval London within the city walls. Common sense tells us that Wallace was brought into the city from the north, perhaps through either Newgate or Bishopsgate, and as Fenchurch is on the route through the old city heading towards the Tower, we can imagine how the procession designed to humiliate Wallace could simply go no further, with the press of the crowd too great, and had to stop here at Fenchurch. Why would they be heading for the Tower? Well, as stated, lists of prisoners include Wallace's name. He was obviously expected in London on 22 August, and his trial was set for the following day. So it makes sense that a cell would have been set aside for Wallace within the Tower.

What thoughts must have gone through his head, chained within that house in Fenchurch? How badly roughed up would he have been? Not just from the ill treatment of the guards, but from missiles thrown by the mob. He seems to have been in a reasonable state in Westminster Hall the next morning, as he was able to make comments in reply to the charges, but then Wallace was a man inured to hardships. He had slept out in all weathers, but had to be ready to fight at a moment's notice. He obviously had a belief in himself, and in the cause he had dedicated his life to. He does not seem like a man who would have easily succumbed to self-pity.

Wallace would perhaps have got a little fitful rest, before awakening to his last day on Earth. Would he have known what was to come? The outcome of his sham trial had obviously already been decided, and his captors may have sneeringly informed him that this was to be his final journey, no less than he deserved, a beggarly Scot who had defied the magnanimity of English Edward.

When taken outside the next morning, Wallace found that he was to be part of a procession through the streets to the place of his 'trial' – Westminster Hall. Westminster Hall is the original and oldest part of the complex of buildings that forms the Houses of

Parliament, which are sometimes called the Palace of Westminster, though the former title seems to be the one that most people use. William Rufus, son of William the Conqueror, began construction of Westminster Hall in the 1080s.

The cavalcade included Wallace's escort through England, John de Segrave. Segrave's brother, Geoffrey, was also in attendance. His 'judges' for the trial ahead were all there. Peter Mallory, justiciar of England, was the leading legal figure. Mallory was to condemn other Scots figureheads in the future during the campaigns of Bruce, most notably Bruce's brother-in-law Christopher Seton. Seton was executed in Dumfries on an eminence now known as the Chrystal or Christol Mount, from Christopher's nickname. It is where St Mary's Church stands today. He also passed sentence on Alexander Scrymgeour, a man who Wallace is said to have befriended at school in Dundee, and who Wallace left in charge of the assault on the English-held castle of Dundee whilst he himself fought and won at Stirling Bridge. Wallace appointed Scrymgeour the standard bearer of the army of Scotland, and Scrymgeour bravely flew the Lion Rampant banner at Wallace's back on the field of battle. After the murder of Wallace he joined Bruce, who gave the standard-bearer appointment the royal seal of approval and made it hereditary. But Scrymgeour was captured and suffered the same hideous fate as Wallace at Newcastle. Mallory also condemned John Strathbogie, the Earl of Atholl.

Another member of the legal profession joined Mallory; the judge Ralph de Sandwych, constable of the Tower of London, who would later sentence Wallace's companion Sir Simon Fraser to death. Fraser's severed head was spiked alongside Wallace's on London Bridge. The mayor of London, John le Blunt, who was obviously there to represent the City of London itself, joined these two, as did John de Bacwell, who eventually met a strange death. When he attended the coronation of Edward II in February 1308, Bacwell was crushed by the press of the crowd and suffocated. Bizarre indeed.

Many aldermen of the city, and some sheriffs, accompanied these four, along with the two Segraves. They made their way to

Westminster Hall, strangely following the route through the city and out towards Charing Cross that Wallace was to be drawn along in the opposite direction only an hour or two later.

There has been debate among historians as to whether Wallace and Longshanks ever came face to face in London. One account says that Longshanks turned his back on Wallace and refused to look at him, but it is doubtful whether they crossed paths. Perhaps each managed to discern the other at a distance at the Battle of Falkirk in 1298 – Wallace, the young giant, urging on his men with the Lion Rampant at his back; Edward Longshanks at the other side of the boggy loch formed by the Westquarter Burn, astride a warhorse and encased in mail and armour, the Leopards of England marking his position, surrounded by a body of knights. I'm sure Wallace would have peered across at his nemesis through narrowed eyes, hoping that if the day went well, he might let the hated invading king test the metal of his blade. Longshanks too would have stared across at Wallace's position and hoped that he would soon have this 'rebel' under his power.

The site of the Houses of Parliament was once an island in the meandering Thames, but drainage and dyke building brought the area into what we could call 'dry land'. Wallace would have looked ahead to Westminster Hall, and Westminster Abbey further over to his right, then been taken from his horse, or horse drawn transport, and hustled inside. It seems the proceedings immediately went ahead, no time wasted on niceties or formalities. The Hall was probably packed. Wallace was placed on a dais at the southern end of the hall. The site is today marked by a little plaque set into the floor. It reads: 'Near this spot, at the Kings Bench at the south end of the Hall, took place the trial of Sir William Wallace, the Scottish Patriot, on Monday 23 August 1305.'

This plaque, made of brass, was unveiled on 31 October 1924, and owes its existence to the diligence of John Robertson, then Labour MP for Bothwell. He had been showing some Scots children from his constituency around Westminster, and their enquiries made him think about marking the spot in some way. There is a plain copy, actual size, of this plaque set into one of the panels of the Wallace monument at his birthplace in Elderslie, Renfrewshire. I have stood upon the original and looked at the view down the hall as Wallace did. The present, impressive hammer-beam roof was not put in place until the late 1300s, but apparently the roof in Wallace's day had some pillars supporting it, and there was a gallery that ran right around its base. This would have been packed with spectators. But the hall is still as recognisable to us as it would have been to Wallace. It is quite a weird sensation to stand on the spot where Wallace himself stood during his final hours. As a Scot I feel the link with my countryman. He would never have been able to envisage me standing there seven centuries on, was never to know if the term 'Scotsman' would still be in use long after he was gone. He would probably be surprised to know that his martyrdom helped to hammer us into recognising the 'Scottishness' inherent within us. For a few seconds I was able to stand on that spot and glimpse a little of what went on inside his head.

As he stood looking out on the scene, a laurel leaf circlet was placed on his head like a crown. This was done in mockery, as the story had been circulated that Wallace had once boasted that he would one day wear the English crown in that very hall. This seems like nonsense, as it does not fit with what we know of the character of Wallace, but it probably shows the route of the propaganda issued by England to discredit him. Wallace apparently removed the laurel leaves from his head, but they were replaced and he was warned to let them be. With a shrug he acceded. This wearing of a mock crown of sorts is reminiscent of Christ's crown of thorns. When Sir Simon Fraser, companion of Wallace, was captured after joining Robert the Bruce's party, he was forced to wear a similar crown of periwinkles. It seems that it was done as another way of belittling those who challenged England's power.

Then Wallace's 'trial' began. As he was regarded as an outlaw, beyond the bounds of the law, he was not allowed to answer or plead 'yea' or 'nay' to any of the charges. The verdict was a forgone conclusion. The charge sheet was a lengthy one. Wallace was charged with robbery, sacrilege, rebellion, sedition, homicide and arson, among other crimes. The slaying of Heselrig, the Sheriff of

Lanark, was mentioned. The fact that he had invaded England was read out to the horrified crowd. One charge was that he had 'flown banners in the field against the King of England.' It seems that, at least for a while, the blue and white Saltire and the Lion Rampant of Scotland flew in defiance of Edward's might. But when the charge of treason was read out, making Wallace a traitor to England, Wallace managed to shout out above the din that he could never be a traitor. He had never sworn allegiance to Edward or England. He was a Scot, and he would not stand idly by at such an accusation. So we know that Wallace still held onto his pride.

However, Edward had taken the surrender of the King of Scots, John Balliol, in 1296, and saw this as the surrender of every individual in Scotland, and thus was dismissive of Wallace's argument. As far as Edward was concerned, Scotland was rightfully his, and the court chose to ignore Wallace's right as a citizen of Scotland to protect his country's nationhood. A scribe was present in the court, taking notes of the trial. The ledger still exists. It was on a short loan to the Museum of Scotland and I saw it there. It was leather bound, but looked strangely modern in layout. It was lined with a margin, not looking so very different to modern A4 ruled paper, although the lines were drawn on by ink and ruler. It was a strange artefact to look at in its glass case. Wallace himself stood before the man who took those notes. Sometimes centuries compress, and the link is there.

Sir John Segrave stood to read the sentence of the court:

And that for the robberies, homicides and felonies he committed in the realm of England and in the land of Scotland [notice Scotland is only referred to as a land, and not a realm like England] *to be there hanged and afterwards taken down from the gallows. And in as much as he was an outlaw, and was not afterwards restored to the peace of the Lord King, he be decollated while he yet lives before being decapitated, and that thereafter, for the measureless turpitude of his deeds towards God's Holy Church, in burning down churches, the heart, the liver, the lungs and all the internal organs of William's body, whence such perverted thoughts proceeded, be removed out of his person and cast into the fire and burnt. Furthermore and finally, that in as much as it was not only against the Lord King himself, but against the whole community of England and of Scotland, the body of the said William be cut up and divided into four parts, that the head, so cut off, be set up on London Bridge, in the sight of such as pass by, whether by land or by water, and that one quarter be hung on a gibbet at Newcastle upon Tyne, another quarter at Berwick, a third quarter at Stirling and the fourth at St Johnstone [Perth] as a warning and deterrent to all that pass by and behold them.*

Wallace would have stared straight ahead, stony faced, as the sentence was read, and I'm sure the hubbub in the hall faded into the background of his mind. The sentence was to be carried out immediately, and he would have been grabbed and pulled from his position within seconds. Wallace's time for glory had come.

CHAPTER FIVE

The Route Through London

WE KNOW THAT WALLACE was sentenced to be dragged through the streets of London to his place of execution, and we are given a little detail from the extant records. We know he was to be taken from Westminster Hall – which at that time stood outwith London, the city being away to the east – to the Tower; from the Tower to the Aldgate; then back through the city to the Elms. Looking at the old maps of the city, I realised that the street lines have not really altered over the centuries, and the road layout within the original old city walls is as it was in Wallace's day.

As already stated, on 22 August 1305 the officials concerned were unable to imprison Wallace for the night in the Tower of London due to the press of the crowds who had turned out to see the Scottish 'monster'. That suggests to me that, when Wallace was dragged to his death on the twenty-third, he would have been taken down the widest, major streets, and not on the minor roads. The populace was out in force, and minor roads would have been impassable due to the crush. A glance at any medieval map of London shows that there is a direct route all the way from Westminster to the Tower, and this route also clearly exists on modern maps. So using very basic means of deduction, I think it safe to say that this is the route that Wallace was taken during his final hours.

Anyone not familiar with the history of London probably thinks that the names of many of its streets are of a fairly modern derivation. For example, Fleet Street is known, or was until fairly recently, as the centre of the newspaper industry, but the name is ancient and refers to the River Fleet, which flowed down to the Thames here – and still does, though it is tunnelled in now. Fleet Street was called Fleet Street in Wallace's time.

Anyone wanting to follow the route along which Wallace was dragged in 1305, to his martyrdom, and to his place in the hearts of the people of Scotland, is advised to take the London Underground to Westminster and emerge from the tube station underneath the Houses of Parliament into the shadow of the tower that contains the famous bell known as Big Ben. As you walk down towards Parliament Square, with the buildings on your left, the door of Westminster Hall stands on the other side of a small grassy area with a large arched window above it. The hall has been re-clad or faced in a more modern layer of stone that belies the antiquity of this old building, but it is still easy to pick out, standing as it does a little separate from the grouping of the other buildings. I suppose it was through this decorated, old Norman archway that Wallace was dragged, to be tied to the tails of the waiting horses, although it is also possible that he was hustled out a side entrance.

It is on that last day of Wallace's life that our current journey begins. I can't even begin to imagine the horror involved for Wallace, the injustice, the humiliation, the fear; what images he concentrated on to try and focus and to steel himself in some way for what lay ahead. As he was taken out from the hall, he would have seen Westminster Abbey over his left shoulder, although I'm sure that noticing London landmarks was the last thing on his mind – but I want to point out many of the pieces of continuity that are on this route, that we can identify today as having a relevance to Scotland and to London in the time of Wallace.

Westminster Abbey is the burial place of many of England's kings and queens, and Edward Longshanks himself is there, buried in a large rectangular tomb in the Chapel of Edward the Confessor. The only ornamentation upon his tomb is the Latin inscription *Edwardus Primus, Malletus Scotorum Rex, Pactum Serva*, which translates as 'Edward the First, the Hammer of the Scots, Keep Faith.' He may have instigated the Wars of Independence. He may have ordered the murder of Sir William Wallace. He may have ridden over our land. But he never subjugated Scotland. King Robert the Bruce fought on for many years, and the outcome was that he made England recognise that Scotland was a separate nation-state. Edward's people may have thought that he was a hammer to Scotland, but Scotland proved it was an anvil that could take the blows. Wallace and Murray defeated one of Edward's armies at Stirling Bridge in 1297, and in the time of his son, Edward ii's reign, the Scots proved to have the ascendancy. Every time I am in London at Westminster, I make a point of going to see Eddie in his tomb, and I make a point of putting my face to the cold stone and whispering, 'Still here!'. Sometimes I can even hear him birling within!

Nonetheless, Westminster Abbey is a stupendous place to visit for anyone with a love of history. I only wish we had the like in Scotland, something that contains so much of our past. But where English invasions and deprivations did not destroy our churches, we did it ourselves at the time of the Reformation – such a loss.

How was Wallace taken through the streets? The general consensus is that he was tied to a wooden hurdle of some sort, perhaps a triangular framework of timber, with his head at the apex. Certainly there are drawings from the 1600s that show condemned persons being drawn on a wooden sled to their place of execution. But there is an older sketch from 1242 of Sir William de Marisco being taken to the gallows. He is dressed in ordinary garb, a rope round each of his ankles, being dragged behind a horse. He would therefore have been jolted along the streets with little protection. Perhaps that was part of the punishment, as the streets of London in the early part of the 1300s were little more than open sewers. But surely the six miles that Wallace was to endure would have caused injuries that would have resulted in a dead man arriving at the gallows? The jolting over stones, bumps and ruts would have broken bones and stripped the skin from his body. Looking at the whole procedure, it is probable that some sort of frame was used, although it has also been suggested that he was wrapped in cow or horsehide to limit the physical damage incurred during the journey.

The route from Westminster Hall to the Tower follows the contour of the River Thames, and as said, modern streets follow closely the route that Wallace must have been taken. I know this may seem a little strange, but if you follow the route, it makes sense to follow the pavement to the right of the road in front, at least to the Tower of London. I had not really thought about it before, but the three times I have walked this route before writing this, I have always stayed on the right. It seems to allow better access and there are fewer junctions to negotiate, probably because the Thames is not too far away on your right, and most of the things to see are easier to observe from this side. So walk on the right!

You will see that in front of you here at Parliament Square there is a statue of Winston Churchill, another man who was no friend of Scotland; nor would I expect or want him to be. Facing him you turn to your right and cross the road into Parliament Street, which leads on into Whitehall. The Cenotaph stands before you in the middle of the road.

Keep your eyes open for the building called the Banqueting Hall, which is on your right. At the far end of this impressive white coloured building (so many buildings in Whitehall are white) there is a gateway leading to the main door, set back a little from the rest of the building.

Above this doorway you will see there is a bust of Charles I. Charles was the son of James VI of Scotland and I of England, thus a member of the Stewart Dynasty, and also a Scot by birth, for he was born at the Royal Palace in Dunfermline. This palace still stands, ruined but impressive, above Pittencrief Glen and beside Dunfermline Abbey. Beneath the bust of Charles there is an inscription that reads: 'His Majesty King Charles passed through this hall and out of a window nearby over this tablet to the scaffold in Whitehall where he was beheaded 30 January 1649.' The bust of Charles is life size and is immediately recognisable from paintings of the man, sporting the moustache and little goatee beard that seem so familiar. Charles was buried in Windsor, along with his severed head, in a coffin that lies next to that of Henry VIII.

As we walk on from the Banqueting House, we see Nelson's Column towering before us, showing us the location of Trafalgar Square. This was countryside in Wallace's day. The edge of the City of London, marked by its town wall, was still further to the north east.

We come to Trafalgar Square, but actually just skirt it to its right, and turn into the Strand, which is found at about two o' clock to your current position. From here to the Tower of London – the best part of three miles away – the street names may change but it is one continuous route. Sometimes the route stretches straight ahead of you, the buildings on either side making it seem as if you are walking down a canyon.

Just a little up the Strand, Charing Cross Station is on your right. In the small car park in front of the station entrance there is a strange rocket-shaped memorial, inlaid with statues, and at a guess about 50ft high. This is an 'Eleanor Cross', and it is from this cross that Charing Cross takes its name. I suppose most Londoners who walk by it on a daily basis are oblivious to what it represents, or the history involved in this stone monument. Its story is tied up with Wallace's great adversary, Edward Longshanks. Edward's first wife was Eleanor of Castile. She died in Harby in Lincolnshire in 1290, and apparently, strange as it seems, Edward was devastated by her death. He was not exactly renowned for his chivalry towards women, and he is remembered for the bestial behaviour he inflicted upon the women of Robert the Bruce in particular, who were displayed in cages like animals, in an attempt to bring the Hero-King of Scots to his knees. Anyway, as Eleanor's body was carried to its last resting place at Westminster Abbey, her funeral procession stopped overnight in twelve places, and Edward of England decided to have twelve crosses erected to mark where his wife's body lay during those stops. Those twelve places were Lincoln, Grantham, Stamford, Geddington, Northampton, Stony Stratford, Woburn, Dunstable, St Albans, Waltham Cross, Westcheap and finally here at Charing Cross. There are only three of the original crosses still standing: the ones at Waltham Cross, Northampton and Geddington. The cross before you here is a copy of the original, which was finished in 1291, but for some reason removed in 1647. The replica that stands today was created by Edward Middleton Barry and was erected in 1863. The original cross would have been in place as Wallace was dragged past. It had been *in situ* 14 years before Wallace's last day.

The name 'Charing' preceded the cross of course, the 'cross' being added only after the Eleanor Cross was built. The cross itself would have been a well-known landmark in the relatively open country between Westminster and the City. 'Charing' is an Old English word denoting a river bend, and as any map of the area shows, the Thames turns sharply here. Charing Cross just means 'the cross by the bend in the river.'

We continue on – a little further along the Strand you will see the Savoy Theatre and the entrance to the Savoy Hotel. Further on again and Savoy Street runs downhill on your right to the River Thames. If you go down Savoy Street here, you only need to walk a few yards and the Savoy Chapel appears on your right. It is a long, low building with a little bell tower. Just round by the tower is the entrance. The chapel is open 11.30 till 3.30, Tuesday till Friday. Perhaps I should tell you why so many places in this area bear the name Savoy. The manor that used to stand on this spot was granted by Henry III of England (the father of Longshanks) to Count Peter of Savoy in 1246. Although Savoy is on the shores of Lake Geneva, the name remained and this area has been called Savoy ever since.

John of Gaunt built a magnificent palace here, but it was destroyed during Wat Tyler's Peasants' Revolt of 1381. Henry viii had a large hospital built on the ruins of the palace in 1512, for 'pouer, nedie people.' It boasted three chapels, and the one that has survived is the chapel before you. But what is the Scottish connection here? If you enter the chapel and walk up to the high altar at the far end, you will notice that to the right of the altar a little brass plate is set into the floor. It reads: 'In memory of Dr Archibald Cameron, brother of Donald Cameron of Locheil, who having been attainted after the Battle of Culloden in 1746, escaped to France but returning to Scotland was apprehended and executed in 1753. He was buried beneath the altar of this chapel.'

Archie was a talented physician who had studied at the University of Edinburgh, and afterwards at Paris, finishing at Leyden in Holland. Although he could have 'set up shop' in any European capital, he returned to his native Lochaber and acted as doctor to his own people. When Bonnie Prince Charlie landed in 1745, Archie's elder brother, Cameron of Locheil, joined the Prince's cause. Archie became the Prince's physician. Eyewitnesses reported that in battle, Archie attended to both friend and foe, showing no partiality when it came to treating the wounded. After Culloden, Archie escaped to France on the same ship as the Prince. He returned to Lochaber in 1753 on Jacobite business, but was arrested on 20 March by Redcoats acting on the intelligence of Hanoverian spies. Archie was conveyed to London, where he was tried and told that he was to be confined in the Tower till 7 June, whereupon 'your body is to be drawn on a sledge to the place of execution, there to be hanged, but not until you are dead, your bowels to be taken out, your body quartered, your head cut off and affixed at the King's disposal, and the Lord have mercy on your soul.' Sound familiar? The English idea of punishment for 'treason' had not changed for the better over the centuries. The fact that Prince Charles Edward Stuart was the rightful heir to the throne of both Scotland and England did not enter the equation.

Archie was placed on a sledge and was pulled by horses to Tyburn, the scene of so many London executions. It is reported that he had a very tearful leave-taking with his wife, who was pregnant with their eighth child. En route, he looked much at the spectators in houses and on balconies, and bowed to several acquaintances. On arrival at Tyburn, he is reported to have said 'Tis my new birthday! There are more witnesses at this birth than at my first.' He then informed the various personages officiating that 'I have now done with this world, and am ready to leave it', and asked them to proceed with haste. He was stood on a cart with the rope round his neck, and the cart drew from beneath him. The body, after hanging for twenty minutes, was cut down but not quartered, although his heart was taken out and burnt. I have never been able to ascertain why his death was different from the sentencing of the court, but poor Archie! His heart taken out and burnt. He had been a man who had tended the sick, and had done his best for the royal line of Scotland. It is reported that: 'On the following Sunday, the remains of Dr Cameron were interred in a vault in the Savoy

Chapel.' Originally there was no marker to him, but later the little plaque was put in place by some 'concerned gentlemen'.

When I first visited the Savoy chapel, I got there at 11.20am. Noticing that it opened at 11.30, I hung round with my daughter, Kimberley, waiting for it to open. Although it is just off the Strand, it stands in a relatively quiet little street. A solitary pedestrian appeared. I recognised him at once as I have attended several speaking engagements with him. It was Jamie, the Earl of Mar and Kellie. It was strange that I was waiting to get in to see the last resting place of the man who was the final tragic victim to be executed in the cause of Jacobitism, when here was the direct descendent of the man who led the Jacobite forces at Sheriffmuir in 1715. Funny old world. We chatted for a few minutes and he went on his way. And the Earl of Mar is not the only connection with Jacobitism hereabouts, as you will see.

Back onto the Strand we cross over Lancaster Place. You will notice that ahead of you there is a church on an island in the middle of the road. This is St Mary le Strand, and if you are lucky it may be open. Sometimes it is open when I have passed, sometimes it isn't. It is quite an impressive place to walk into. The altar at the far end is quite spectacular. Above are blue stained glass windows that replaced originals damaged by bomb blasts during the Second World War. The church building itself was designed by James Gibbs and completed in 1717.

Now the following may come as a bit of a surprise to those who have believed or have been brought up on the propaganda that Bonnie Prince Charlie was an effete, lisping dandy who abandoned his people after the Battle of Culloden. Although there was a price on his head, and capture would have meant certain execution, Charles turned up in London just four years after Culloden to try and gauge public support for the Stuart cause. Though Charles has often been depicted by his detractors as a staunch Roman Catholic who led a Catholic 'revolt', he was actually very tolerant where religion was concerned and the army who had followed him from Glenfinnan in 1745 was mostly Episcopalian. Legend tells us that it was here in St Mary le Strand that Charles converted to

Protestantism in 1750, and so you can stand in this ornate building and imagine Charles standing before the Anglican minister taking his vows. It seems extraordinary that Charles managed to arrive in London incognito, but he must have had quite a few sympathisers who were prepared to cover for him. The fact that word of this visit never reached the ears of the Hanoverian regime is quite amazing. But Charles did have the blood of Robert the Bruce flowing through his veins, and perhaps he inherited his courage too.

Back over to the right hand side of the Strand and we continue. You will see there is another church on an island in the middle of the road beyond St Mary's. This is St Clement Danes. This church is on an ancient site and takes its name from the fact that Danes worshipped here in the ninth century at the time of Alfred the Great. I remember I had to learn this rhyme when I was at school:

> *Oranges and lemons, say the bells of St Clement's,*
> *You owe me five farthings, say the bells of St Martin's,*
> *When will you pay me, say the bells of Old Bailey,*
> *When I grow rich, say the bells of Shoreditch,*
> *When will that be, say the bells of Stepney,*
> *I do not know, says the great bell of Bow.*

Sometimes at the end two extra lines are added:

> *Here comes a candle to light you to bed*
> *Here comes a chopper to chop off your head*

And sometimes even a third:

> *Chip, chop, chip, chop, the last man is dead.*

St Clement Danes' bells do indeed play the melody that has been translated into the words 'Oranges and Lemons', although this also applies to St Clement's in Eastcheap, so there is debate about which is the church mentioned in the rhyme. But the reason

I mention this is because much of the route that Wallace was taken runs through the oldest parts of London and you may hear the toll of some of these bells as you walk the route. The lines that are sometimes added at the end obviously refer to capital punishment and executions in London, and so it is all tied in with our story here. It has never ceased to amaze me the way that history interlinks, but I should not be surprised as history is of course the glue that binds us all together.

The current St Clement Danes was designed by Christopher Wren, and completed in 1680. It was damaged badly during a bombing raid in the Second World War, but was rebuilt. But an earlier version stood here as Wallace was drawn past, and I find myself constantly on this walk casting my mind back to 1305 and imagining his final journey. As you draw level with the rear of St Clement Danes, and the Royal Courts of Justice – a large impressive building – appears to your left, you will notice that Essex Street is the thoroughfare on your right. If you walk down Essex Street just seven or eight yards, there is a plaque set into the wall on the right hand side. This plaque is in remembrance of Essex House, which stood here, and there is a list of the important personages who stayed there. You will notice it says that Prince Charles Edward Stuart was there in 1750. With Archie's last resting place in the Savoy Chapel, St Mary le Strand, and this plaque mentioning Charles, it is quite amazing to have so many Jacobite connections in such a short space of the route.

A little further along the Strand and we come to the Temple Bar. It stands in the middle of road and is in the form of a large pedestal surmounted by a dragon or griffin. There was originally a bar or chain across the way here, used as a tollgate, and it marked the edge of the jurisdiction of the City of London. The reason it was called 'Temple Bar' is because of its proximity to the Temple Church, the headquarters of the Knights Templar in England. Temple Bar is first mentioned in 1301, so there was a barrier of sorts here as Wallace was taken through in 1305, which was probably opened for the purpose. It also shows once again that the route of the road from Wallace's day has not deviated.

Christopher Wren built a gateway here in the 1600s, but it was removed and the site is marked by the current monument. The monument marks the spot where the Strand becomes Fleet Street. Just after the monument, keep your eyes peeled for the sign that points the way down a little alley on your right to Temple Church. There is an oasis of calm in the little square here, somehow inured to the hustle and bustle of the huge city stretching out in every direction around you – for most of its history the biggest city on the planet. In the words of that great biographer of London, Peter Ackroyd, the trees here are full of 'smokey sparrows playing at country', a line that made me laugh, as that was exactly how I perceived it!

The Temple Church was built in its round style in acknowledgement of the Church of the Holy Sepulchre in Jerusalem, and was consecrated in 1185. The Church of the Holy Sepulchre was of course the holiest of the holy to the Crusaders, and it was to that church that Robert the Bruce wished to have his heart presented before its return to Melrose Abbey in the Scottish Borders. The interior of London's Temple Church is well worth a visit though, as there are nine life-size effigies of knights within. Many are from the 1200s and so are depicted in the armour of the period. It is possible to get an idea of the accoutrements of the battlefield from Wallace's time. Shields, swords, chain mail and war helms; even the strapping required is well depicted on the better-preserved tombs. It is so interesting to remember that after the Battle of Falkirk in 1298, Sir Brian le Jay, the Master of the English Templars, was slain as he tried to follow the Scots into the cover of Callendar Wood. Some have said that it was Wallace himself who dispatched him with a sweep of his mighty sword. Strange then, that Wallace should pass their headquarters on his final journey.

On with our journey – the straight road ahead now is Fleet Street. Look for No. 143 on your left hand side. This is a strange one indeed! The building is currently an eatery called Pret a Manger. You will notice it has a life size-ish statue of Mary Queen of Scots at first floor level, and it actually has written on its front 'Mary Queen of Scots' House, 1582 – 1587.' Now, Mary Queen of

Scots never visited London, at least while she was still alive. After she was confined by her English captors, she was kept at several locations, but all were north of here. When she died she was first buried at Peterborough Cathedral, but when James vi inherited the throne of England she was exhumed and reburied in Westminster Abbey. So she is now in London, although not in this house! I am intrigued as to how this building has gained the appellation of 'Mary Queen of Scots' House' as no record I have seen says that she was ever there. Nice to see the Scottish connection though, and nice to see a statue of Mary. After all, the English had her beheaded for treason and a monarch of one country cannot be guilty of treason against the monarch of another.

As you proceed along Fleet Street the dome of St Paul's Cathedral will start to appear in the distance, sitting on its slightly elevated site. The old London of its early days was built upon two hills, Ludgate Hill and Cornhill, and though the whole area is now a mass of buildings you can still detect their slight rising above the streets around. They are not like the hills that abound in our Scottish cities, the hills that our urban streets climb in Glasgow, Dundee or Edinburgh – hills that give a right good burn to the calves of many a cyclist – but you can detect them nonetheless. Fleet Street leads on to Ludgate Circus, a circular ring of buildings surrounding a busy crossroads. The name Ludgate comes from the old gate here, the westernmost gate of the wall that surrounded the city. The Romans built the first wall around London, and it was built even higher in medieval times. There are many remnants of the old wall, but not at this side of the city. There is actually a London Wall Walk that is about a mile and three-quarters long, with storyboards pointing out the details of the most important sites, but this is more to the east and north of the old city boundary. The street named London Wall is a good guide to the remains, with many remnants between modern buildings just to the north side of that thoroughfare.

But Ludgate is an important stage on Wallace's last journey, as this is where he would have been dragged into the city proper. I can blot out the modern hubbub, the noise of the traffic, and picture the old stone gateway here, flanked by its towers. Although the route so far would have led through hamlets, and by churches like the Temple, it was here that Wallace actually entered London. Here is where the crowds would have begun to press in at either side of the road. There would probably have been many atop the walls and atop the towers of the Ludgate itself who would have let out a cry at the approach of the 'traitorous Scot.' Was Wallace in any condition by this time to have been aware that he passed through the walls and into the city? I suppose it depends on how he was conveyed, whether he was simply dragged behind horses or on a sledge or a wooden frame of some sort. But for me the sounds of modern London recede and I hear the baying of the crowd, and the hero of Scotland gets dragged by, and they close in his passing, and yelling, follow his path as a horde.

We cross Ludgate Circus and are now walking up Ludgate Hill, sloping up towards St Paul's. It would originally have been ground rising away above the River Fleet. At the top of Ludgate Hill, St Paul's looms large before you. The main entrance faces you here. Most folk know that this huge edifice was constructed by Sir Christopher Wren after the Great Fire of London in 1666, but it is built on the site of an earlier building. It stands huge and overpowering above the city when you see it on old landscape drawings of London. The first church here – constructed of wood – was erected in AD 604. It burnt to the ground and was replaced between 675 and 685, but this version was destroyed in 962 by a Viking raiding party. Strange to think of Viking longships drawn up on the Thames and the warriors they despatched running riot through these streets.

The huge medieval version of St Paul's took 150 years to complete, the finishing touches being applied in 1240. It was this church that Wallace was taken by in 1305. The church had a Gothic Choir added in 1313, which made it the longest church in Europe at 596ft. A spire was added the following year, 1314, the year of Bannockburn, and at 489ft it was the tallest in Europe. As the rubble of this old St Paul's was sifted after the Great Fire a stone was found which bore the word 'resurgam', which means 'I shall rise again.' It is carved into the pediment of the south door, beneath a phoenix. St Paul's has risen again and again from all the ravages of the centuries, not unlike the memory of Wallace in the people of Scotland.

The road swings a little round the south side of St Paul's and here it takes on the title of St Paul's Churchyard, which I suppose this was at one time. As we get to the rear of St Paul's, the name changes to Cannon Street. If you are reading this without knowing the route, all these name changes must make it seem very confusing and complicated, but each street leads directly onto the next, and walking this long stage of Wallace's journey eastwards is very straightforward. We follow Cannon Street on, and after a while Queen Victoria Street runs across at an angle. You will notice signs for the College of Arms pointing down this street. There is another Scottish connection here. The College of Arms is the English equivalent of the Lord Lyon's office in Scotland. In other words, it is where heraldic coats of arms are listed and conferred. And within this building reside the sword, ring and dagger taken from King James iv's body after he was slain at the Battle of Flodden in 1513. I covered the story of these relics in my book *A Passion for Scotland*. I know that to the English these items will be seen as spoils of war, as Flodden was fought on English soil. But I feel that they would draw many curious sightseers in a Scottish museum, which would be better than their being tucked up in a building in London where interest in them is marginal. After all, it was that very ring, a gift to James from the Queen of France, with a note beseeching him to advance into England, which was responsible for the slaughter of perhaps 10,000 Scots on Flodden's field. Certainly I, and I'm sure many other Scots, would like to be able to go and see these pieces whenever we wished; they should be displayed in a Scottish museum.

Further along Cannon Street, look for Cannon Street Station on your right hand side. Just opposite the station there is a building housing the OCBC bank. Look for the little grill, almost like an old fireplace, set into the front of the bank at street level. Behind this grill stands London Stone. I wanted to include this relic in this walk, as it has echoes of our very own Stone of Destiny in its story. The London Stone is formed from oolite, a form of limestone. It may have been larger at one time, and may have been broken, or perhaps chipped away when it was on public display over the centuries. There is a little plaque above the stone, which reads: 'This is a fragment of the original piece of limestone once securely fixed in the ground now fronting Cannon Street Station, removed in 1742 to the north side of the street, in 1798 it was built into the south wall of the church of St Swithin Londunston, which stood here until demolished in 1962. Its origin and purpose are unknown, but in 1188 there was a reference to Henry, son of Eylwin de Londenstane, subsequently the Lord Mayor of London.' There are many stories and legends surrounding the stone. One is that it was formerly a druid altar, but the most widely believed is that the Stone was brought to London by Brutus of Troy, after the collapse of that city. This has parallels with the Stone of Destiny, Jacob's Pillow, being brought from the Middle East by the Scots. But there is also the opinion that it was originally a marker set up by the Romans, and that all distances along their roads were calculated from this stone. We know of similar stones in cities in other Roman-conquered lands, with all distances calculated from that particular point. The first written reference we have of it is for the early part of the first century AD, with some lands and rents referred to as being 'neer unto London stone.' The stone certainly became an important landmark, where proclamations were made and laws were passed.

In the time of Henry VI of England, who was an unpopular king, there was a revolt led by one Jack Cade. He marched an army into London, paused at London Stone and struck it with his sword, declaring himself Lord Mayor of London. This too has parallels with the crowning process on the Stone of Destiny. It was obviously much revered over the centuries, and was a talisman of the people of London, yet it seems to have faded from their memory in the pace of the modern city. Several times in Scotland when taking photos, people have stopped and looked nonplussed at my subject matter, and the same thing happened here. As I crouched taking photos, passers-by stopped, looked at me, looked at the stone and looked at me again. As I walked on I could see a little group peering at this lump of stone and wondering why that man was taking photos of it!

Onwards on Cannon Street till we cross King William Street, which leads down to the modern London Bridge on our right. This next section really moved me when I put the details together, especially when it all fell into place as I was standing there.

I, being ignorant of the details, was visiting London one time and was trying to find out the exact site of the original London Bridge from Wallace's day. I had been lucky enough to glean passes for the Tower of London from two lady members of the Society of William Wallace who were from Liverpool. It had been raining; I was in denims and was pretty thoroughly soaked, as I had been doing my usual walking about trying to absorb my surroundings and not worrying too much about the weather. I am Scottish and used to bracing wet weather, after all! Anyway, in the Tower I was taking photos and scrambling about quite a bit, and eventually I came to the attention of the Beefeaters, the curiously dressed guards who work in the Tower. I asked some of them if they could tell me where the old London Bridge stood, the one covered in buildings depicted on so many old scenes of London. 'Why do you want to know?' asked one of them, looking at my unkempt and dripping state. 'I'm an author and historian', I replied. 'If you're a historian, I'm Ghengis Khan', he retorted. 'Well, Ghengis', I replied, 'where exactly was the old London Bridge situated?' Strangely, none of the three Beefeaters around me had any idea. I assumed that they would have knowledge of their city's history. I found out eventually, though, that the original London Bridge where Wallace's head was spiked and displayed lay just a few yards downstream from the modern one.

Continue along, and once you have passed the aforementioned King William Street, you find yourself on Eastcheap. As you come to Fish Street Hill on your right, you can see the tall monument built to commemorate the great Fire of London in 1666, some 50 metres down the road. It has a gold coloured sculpture of flames emanating from its top. People in London refer to it simply as 'The Monument'. It became noted for the amount of people who used to throw themselves from it to commit suicide, as there is a viewing gallery running round its top. It is enclosed with wire now, just in case you fancy doing likewise. Apparently, it stands as tall as the exact distance it stands from the site of the house in Pudding Lane where the fire actually started. Wallace's route takes us by the point where the fire began, and also where the fire was finally extinguished, so we will return to the subject of the Great Fire.

I want you to deviate from the route just a little, to show you what I found so poignant. Walking down to and past the monument brings us to busy Lower Thames Street, and you will notice that there is a church here on the far side. This is the church of St Magnus the Martyr. As you approach the entrance of this church you will notice it has a blue plaque on its front wall. It is one of the famous London 'Blue Plaques' that you will see in many places in the city, pointing out sites of mostly historical or literary interest. This one informs that the small stretch of cobbles in front of the church is the approach to old London Bridge. With a start I realised that after Wallace's execution, the cart containing his head would have passed by the entrance to St Magnus and onto the bridge. Just for a minute all the traffic noise faded and I could see the cart rolling by, a few armed men in attendance, en route to sticking their grisly memento on a spike above the drawbridge that all visitors to London approaching from the south had to cross. They would look up at the heads there, with their sightless eyes, and marvel at the justice of the King of England. I was standing where the head of Wallace had passed nearly 700 years before, still warm from his 'judicial' murder.

The cobbles that led on to London Bridge come to an abrupt halt today, as there is a modern-ish building between the church and the river, but at least you now know the location of the bridge, though it is long gone. It was built in 1126, and believe it or not, it survived until 1831. As you can see from many old drawings, it was covered in buildings, even a church, and for a long time it had a latrine conveniently placed above the swift flowing Thames.

Before we walk round to the spot on the bank of the Thames where the bridge actually stood, I hope you can gain access to the church of St Magnus the Martyr. It is open 10AM till 4PM, Tuesday to Friday. In the foyer of the church is a remarkable model of old London Bridge by David T. Agget. It is very large and you can see clearly where the heads are spiked above the gatehouse. It will give you a good insight into how this area once looked. Incidentally, the St Magnus who gave his name to this church is St Magnus of Orkney, the same who gave his name to St Magnus's Cathedral in Kirkwall! He was martyred in 1116.

The obvious thing to do now is walk round to the bank of the Thames, as you now have an indication from the remains of the access road at St Magnus's as to the actual site of the bridge. The current London Bridge is a little upstream from the site. I suppose Wallace's head would have been dipped in pitch to preserve it before it was hoisted on a long pole that was used to display such trophies. It would eventually have rotted, and either dropped onto the bridge or fallen into the Thames below. We do not know what became of it. I once had someone contact me with the suggestion of dredging the river at this point to see what came up, but I had to gently point out that many hundreds, perhaps thousands, of heads were displayed in such a manner over the centuries. Wallace's head, in fact, was joined by that of Sir Simon Fraser, one of his comrades-in-arms, only a few months after his execution. A German visitor to London in 1598 recorded being able to count more than 30 heads spiked on the bridge as he rode under the gatehouse. Even if a skull was found in that river, who would be able to declare it that of Wallace? Yet I have stood on the riverbank and gazed across the Thames at the point where the old bridge stood, watching the dark waters slide past. Most rivers are seen in feminine terms, yet the Thames seems essentially masculine. 'Old Father Thames' is how he is affectionately known to Londoners. The essence of the mind that gave victory at Stirling Bridge, and hope to all those millions of Scots over the centuries who wanted control over their own destinies, is out there. Perhaps in that river are just a few grains of the element of the person who once lived and breathed Scotland. But we have to drag ourselves away from the waterside, where we can see Tower Bridge further downstream – indicating the proximity of the Tower of London, which it stands beside – and onwards on our route back on Eastcheap.

The next street along on your right is Pudding Lane, where the Great Fire of London started in 1666. A little further and the street name again changes, this time to Great Tower Street, and here you can discern the Tower of London ahead of you. Fenchurch Street is to the north of you here, and so it was somewhere not too far from you that Wallace was incarcerated the night before his journey.

At the far end of Great Tower Street there is a bar on your right named, strangely, The Hung, Drawn and Quartered. I recommend you cross over to the left side of the road here, with the church of All Hallows by the Tower directly in front. We are now on Byward Street, and walking onwards with the Tower to our right. Byward Street soon becomes Tower Hill as we draw level with the Tower itself. The slight rise here above the Tower does not really seem to be enough to merit the description of 'hill', or at least by Scottish standards it does not seem much of a hill. But this indeed is the Tower Hill where so many executions of Scots, amongst others, took place. After the collapse of the '45 in Scotland, for example, Lords Kilmarnock and Balmerino were beheaded here in front of huge crowds. The axe and block used are preserved in the Tower of London, as is the Lochaber Axe, which was used to slay Colonel Gardner, the Hanoverian commander, in the Battle of Prestonpans in 1745. Simon Fraser, Lord Lovat, head of the Fraser Clan, was also executed here for his part in the Jacobite uprising of 1745 (I hate to see the word 'rebel' used in this context, as Charlie was the true heir). At the time of his execution, he was 80 years old. Many prisoners held within the Tower were executed on Tower Hill over the centuries. Excavations here have revealed the remains of a Roman settlement that was burned by Boudicea, so it seems it has been a place of death for a very long time.

You will also notice as you walk on that there is a section of the old London Wall on your left. The lower courses are Roman, the upper, medieval. You can tell the Roman-built section as it has lines of red tiling running horizontally through it vertically every few feet. I don't really know if this is standard, but every other section of Roman walling I have seen, like the one at Chester for example, has the same red tiling layer within it. Still, the London Wall stood there when Wallace was dragged past. And it was at this point he was taken northwards. You will remember that the sentence said that he had to be drawn from Westminster Hall to the Tower, and from the Tower to Aldgate, then back through the City to Smithfield? Well, the Aldgate was north of here, so Wallace must have been taken by this section of wall.

To continue on our modern day version of his trek, we take the first left after this section of wall, under the railway bridge we can see ahead, and we are on a street called Minories. Strange sounding name, but it comes from the fact that there was a foundation here at one time of the 'Friars Minor', and the name has survived. And as the word 'minor' is the root, it also gives a clue to the pronunciation. This is not a long stretch, and we walk up to the major junction at the top of the road. When you reach this junction, if you look to the right, on the northern side of the street you will see the Underground signs that denote Aldgate tube station. The street running left here is also called Aldgate, and this is of course because this city gate once stood in this vicinity. So we turn left into Aldgate, and I want you to cross the road to the north side as soon as safely possible. There is an information board here that has an artist's impression of how the gate looked. It also tells us that the Romans built the first gate on this site, allowing access through the City Wall. It was rebuilt from 1108 to 1147, and again in 1215, the year of the Magna Carta in England. Geoffrey Chaucer, the famed English writer, once stayed in an apartment over the gate itself, from 1374 onwards. The gate was finally demolished in 1761 in order to improve traffic access. I would imagine that the name is a corruption of 'oldgate'; the Scottish equivalent would be 'auldgate', although it could date back to Roman times, and be of an origin more obscure.

As we head back towards the old city, the road forks. The southern fork is Fenchurch Street, the northern, Leadenhall. The two come back together at Bank tube station. This is the only bit where I am not 100% sure about the route. It could be either, but I feel in my bones the northernmost, Leadenhall, is correct. Going by Fenchurch Street takes us very close to the route that Wallace had already travelled, plus he was kept in this area the night before, and must have been paraded to a certain extent, probably in a cart or on horseback, on his way to Westminster Hall. So I am plumping for the northern route, although I have to say that the two do not differ in direction that greatly, and both are very old thoroughfares. So we walk along Leadenhall, which runs almost due west. Leadenhall's south side is the home to the Lloyds of London building, a modern design that you will either love or hate. Leadenhall leads on to Cornhill, and again there will be a few name changes here, but it is a direct route with street running into street.

Cornhill takes us to the major junction where stand the Royal Exchange and the Bank of England, both imposing and prominent buildings. Cross straight over and into Poultry. This name comes from the fact that poultry was bought and sold here in medieval times. Poultry leads on to Cheapside, with the famous church of Bow on your left. And here on your right is Wood Street. A little up Wood Street, Gresham Street runs across, and Wood Street continues, but there is a slight stagger of the street line. The building directly in front of you on this junction as you walk up Wood Street is owned by Standard Life, an Edinburgh-based company, and stands on the site of the church of St Michael's of Wood Street. It was here that the head of King James IV of Scotland, he who died at Flodden and whose sword, ring and dagger are in the College of Arms, was eventually buried. Again, I covered that story in *A Passion for Scotland*.

I know there is an old tower in the centre of Wood Street, but this has nothing to do with St Michael's, in case you think it a relic of that church. There is more to be read on the subject of James in Stow's book, *A Survey of London*. Stow gives an eyewitness account of London in the year 1598, and it was this account that first put me on the trail of James's whereabouts. St Michael's was a ruin by 1900, and the whole site now lies hidden beneath the inexorable crawl of modern building that constantly recreates London.

Following Cheapside soon brings us to the north side of St Paul's Cathedral. We are now on Newgate Street. The name comes from the notorious prison that bore the name, the staging post for many executions in London – some at the prison itself, some at nearby Smithfield, and many, many thousands at Tyburn to the west. The prison was built in the 1100s, and stood into the 1800s. It was a hell on earth, its early days containing reports of cannibalism within its walls, its later days ones of hideous abuses of both its male and female inmates. All ages and generations agree on the 'terrible vapours' that originated from within its unimaginable depths. The Old Bailey, strangely, I suppose, for a building associated with justice, stands on its site, and you may catch a glimpse of the statue of the Scales of Justice atop its dome, on the left side of the street before you. But the strangest coincidence of the whole route, at least for me, is before us on the right hand side, for here stand the ruins of Christchurch Greyfriars, on the corner of Newgate and King Edward Street. (Yes, I'm afraid it is named after Edward I, Longshanks!)

The place was bombed during the Blitz, and has been ruined ever since, but the steeple and most of one wall have survived and a rose garden has been planted in the body of the old church. It is a little haven in the midst of the traffic of central London, a place where office workers can sit during nicer days and eat their sandwiches. But the ruined church is only the latest incarnation of this site. There was a Franciscan monastery here, built in 1228, which survived till 1306, the year after Wallace was taken past. A church was built to replace this monastery and Margaret, second wife and widow of Edward Longshanks, founded it; it was consecrated in 1325. It is recorded that it contained eleven altars, and the building was paved with marble. It must have been quite a magnificent church, because it became a great favourite of the royalty of that time, almost a mother church to the Plantagenets. As I said, it was the wife of Edward I who founded the place. The wife of his son, Edward II, Queen Isabella, was a great benefactor of it, and their son, Edward III's wife, Queen Phillipa, also granted large sums to this church. The aforementioned Queens Margaret and Isabella were buried in ornate tombs within this church, as were many other people of note.

The church survived intact until Henry viii of England came to the fore. He did not recognise the Pope and began his own church, the Anglican Church; he dissolved the monasteries in 1538, pocketing much of the wealth that these places had accumulated. The ornate interior, along with the tombs, was destroyed. I don't care in what country such selfish destruction takes place; I find it very sorrowful. The remains of the church today are those of yet another constructed by Sir Christopher Wren after the Great Fire of 1666.

Now here is the twist. The Isabella mentioned earlier, and buried within, was the same princess with whom Wallace had an affair in the motion picture *Braveheart*. This affair never actually happened, of course, as she was only a girl of six or so when Wallace was taken on his last journey. The story is much older than *Braveheart*, however, as that venerable old Wallace biographer, Blind Harry, tells the tale of Wallace's with the soon-to-be Queen of England in his book, written in the 1400s. No matter. What I find strange is that Wallace was taken past a religious building that was to be the last resting place of a French princess who was to become Queen of England, and that 690 years later, in 1995, a Hollywood movie was to be released that saw Wallace having an affair with this woman. I don't imagine that any one of us in our wildest dreams could imagine such a scenario taking place so long after our demise, and Wallace would have been no different. It is finding out such bits and pieces of history that makes each and every day an adventure to me. I have stood on the pavement, casting my mind back to his final journey, then turned to look at the church and thought of the funeral procession bringing Isabella to her last resting place, neither of them knowing that their stories would be intertwined in centuries to come. They never clapped eyes on one another in life as far as I know, as at the time of his death she was a young girl in France. Still, Wallace visited France during his travels around 1300. When he was captured he had a safe conduct from the King of France on his person. Is it possible that this brawny warrior saw Isabella when she was just a babe in a cradle? Twists and turns indeed.

We continue on just a little on Newgate Street, and like Ludgate and Aldgate, which we have already visited, Newgate was the name of the gate through the City Walls that once stood here. Wallace would have been taken through this gate and out of the city, as Smithfield stood just beyond the wall. In fact, the wall formed the boundary behind Greyfriars Christchurch, which we have just visited, so the line of the old wall was that close here. We take the last major corner of our journey now, and turn right up Giltspur Street. Once through the New Gate, Wallace would have been taken up the side of St Bartholomew's Hospital grounds to the place of execution. Both St Bartholomew's Hospital and the church of St Bartholomew the Great were founded together, two distinct halves of the one entity, in 1123.

We walk up Giltspur Street, the hospital buildings forming the wall on our right. Halfway up the street you will notice a cherubic looking statue of a boy on an angle on the left at first floor level. He is not difficult to spot, being gold in colour. He is the 'Golden Pyx', and he was erected to mark a spot where the Great Fire came to a halt. The Great Fire, having started in Pudding Lane, was ascribed to the sin of gluttony – that is, when the Papists were not being blamed. So this chubby boy represents that sin.

Before you stands the little cluster of tall trees that mark out West Smithfield, with Smithfield Meat Market beyond. We walk round the corner on our right, and nearby you will see an entrance-way in the Tudor style. This archway takes us into the precincts of the Church of St Bartholomew the Great, which would have been the last thing that Wallace saw. As you walk towards this doorway, you will notice that there is a large granite plaque set into the wall of St Bartholomew's Hospital on your right hand side. This is the memorial to Sir William Wallace. It marks where his final journey came to an end and marks where our journey in his footsteps concludes too.

Unlike the Hero of Scotland, your journey continues. But pause awhile and reflect, traveller. For a man died here once, only a man of flesh and blood. A man in a million, nay, a hundred million, because his name itself is a talisman to his people. Nations only manage to give birth to a few of the like in a millennium. And this was where Wallace moved on to a better place, and to a place in the hearts of the Scottish people.

CHAPTER SIX

St Bart's

THE CHURCH OF ST BARTHOLOMEW the Great is entwined with the final moments of Wallace's life, yet it is probable that he never even heard its name mentioned.

St Bart's, to give it its commonly used nickname, is the oldest surviving church in London, as 84 old churches were destroyed during the Great Fire of 1666. The fire managed to jump the city wall here and there, and did so near Newgate, as the Golden Pyx in Giltspur Street testifies. St Bart's was just far enough away from the press of city buildings, and the wind was blowing in a favourable direction, so it was spared.

There are many legends surrounding the foundation of St Bart's. The man responsible for its being built was one Rahere, who was jester to Henry I of England and his queen, Matilda, a daughter of Malcolm Canmore and St Margaret of Scotland. Rahere decided to go on a pilgrimage to Rome to pray for his sins to be pardoned. While there, he fell ill, and made a vow that if he recovered he would found a hospital and church in London. He did recover and then had a dream connected with his vow. In this dream he was lifted up by a beast with four feet and two wings, which took him to a 'high place'. Here he cowered in terror, but St Bartholomew, one of the twelve apostles, appeared, and told Rahere that he was to found a church and hospital at Smoothfield, now known as Smithfield, just outside the city wall. Rahere returned to London, and asked for an audience with King Henry. He told the King this story, and Henry granted him land that was at that time being used as a graveyard. (It amazes me that people then would quite happily listen to and absorb stories of creatures with four feet and two wings, but times have changed!) And so, in 1123, work began on the building of St Bartholomew the Great.

Like Wallace, St Bartholomew was martyred. He was flayed and crucified, head downward, at Albanopolis in Armenia. Because of his being flayed alive, St Bartholomew is often depicted holding his own skin over his arm, as in Michelangelo's *Last Judgement*. There is a statue of him in the upper part of the gatehouse of St Bart's where he is shown in this way.

Having received the King's permission, Rahere went back to his previous guise as a jester, and, gathering all the local children to him, had them merrily scour London for stones to be used in the construction of the church. People say that St Bart's is the true spirit of London itself, as its stones came from every corner of the city. When the building was complete, it is said a heavenly light shone down from the heavens and bathed the church in its glow for an hour. Miracles were reported. Cripples were healed, the dumb could speak. Rahere was buried within his creation, and a richly decorated tomb was built for him in around 1405. The tomb was opened in June 1866, and Rahere's skeleton was found within a wooden coffin still wearing its leather sandals. St Bartholomew's church and the adjoining hospital became a vital and integral part of medieval London, and many historical events took place in the shadow of its buildings.

1381 saw the Peasants' Revolt in England. The people rose in outrage against the unfair taxes levied on them to pay for the wars against France. A ragtag army was assembled and it marched on London under the leadership of Wat Tyler. Wat came face to face with King Richard ii of England and the Lord Mayor of London, William Walworth, at the west door of St Bart's. (It is this door that forms the archway of the gatehouse that leads in from West Smithfield, now surmounted by the half timbered house that was built above it in 1558.) Wat behaved too familiarly in front of the King for the Lord Mayor's liking, and he drew steel and cut Wat down. Although his army was stationed nearby, the peasants did not realise what had happened and their revolt petered out. Many were executed for their parts, several at Smithfield itself. So as you enter the church precincts you pass the spot where a major incident of English history took place. It could easily have had such a different outcome, which would have drastically changed the history of that country, and perhaps of ours.

The church has changed over the course of its nine centuries, of course; as already mentioned, the gatehouse was once the entrance to the church, but that part has been demolished. Wallace was never inside St Bart's, but that does not detract from any visit to this venerable old place. As you enter, you leave the London of the 21st century behind, and enter a building whose very stones seem to shout the antiquity of the place. You can feel the age of the church; the 900 years that it has existed are tangible. And as I walk in, I feel Wallace's presence here more than I do at many other sites. It is as if some shade of him has stayed behind, as if part of his soul fled for the church as he was being dismembered outside. And why should he not be here in part? It was the last thing that he saw, and the church was reflected in his darkening eyes.

Outside the church was the level ground that gave the place its name: 'Smoothfield.' Standing not far from the city's New Gate, it became the centre for the buying and selling of horseflesh. Everything from ponies to carthorses, horses for ploughing to steeds for the most renowned of knights, could be purchased here. A nearby pool was known as the 'Horse Pool', as it was where the animals were taken to drink. The sales were held every Friday, but on other days Smithfield became a common site for executions. Elm trees once stood here also, and the actual place of execution was for a long time known as Smithfield Elms. Like Smithfield, Tyburn, that other site of London executions, was originally known as Tyburn Elms. Elm trees seem to be associated with places of execution, or were specially chosen to be present at the sites of such. Perhaps it is not so strange when you remember that the Greeks saw the elm tree as a symbol of death, and that to the Normans it was the tree of justice. I have seen it suggested that Wallace was executed at Tyburn, but I have not seen this supported by anything other than conjecture. It does not seem likely that Wallace would have been dragged eastwards toward the City from Westminster, all the way to the Tower, then taken right back through the City westwards again and then through open country a few extra miles out to Tyburn. Tyburn is the area just north of Marble Arch today, and the site of the 'Tyburn Tree' is commemorated by a plaque set flat into a traffic island at the Marble Arch end of Edgware Road. I took photos and slides of this area and it almost became a place of death again as I dodged the hurtling traffic to get out to the plaque! You may also be interested to know that Edgware Road runs on the line of the old Roman road known as Watling Street. Perhaps that is why that particular spot was chosen as a site of execution, as it was positioned at the southern end of one of England's most prominent thoroughfares.

But there is another reason that I do not really have any doubts that Smithfield is the correct site. I had always wondered why Wallace was rushed south to London in only nineteen days, and why, once there, his execution was held the next day, after his hasty 'trial'. A fair grew up around St Bartholomew's Church that was eventually to become the major fair in London, a public holiday no less, when the populace would gather to buy and sell, to revel, and to simply get drunk. St Bartholomew's Fair, vast in size, continued till comparatively recent times. There have even been resurrections of it, albeit on a much smaller scale, over the last few years. As it was St Bartholomew's Fair, it was held around the feast day of the saint. That feast day was 24 August. When I discovered this, things fell into place. Wallace was rushed south, and unlike other 'traitors', he was not thrown into a dank cell in the Tower to rot for several months. He was rushed for execution on 23 August 1305. His hideous murder was to be the opening spectacle of that year's St Bartholomew's Fair. Edward Longshanks was obviously determined to display his power to as many people as possible, and the vast crowds thronging to the medieval fair would see the 'champion' of Scotland torn to pieces, and could marvel at the might of England.

CHAPTER SEVEN

The End

ON ARRIVAL AT SMITHFIELD, Wallace would immediately have been loosened from whatever contraption was used to convey him. The crowds must have been huge. Not only would there have been a large gathering at Smithfield awaiting his arrival, but also many of the crowd lining the streets to see his passing would have run after him to catch the spectacle to come. Many would also have cut through the back streets as he passed, heading towards the Tower, to catch sight of him again on his journey back through the City from the Aldgate. It was St Bartholomew's Fair, and along with the many vendors, sideshows, stalls and farmyard animals for sale, there was the added attraction of seeing this Scottish ruffian, who had dared to face up to King Edward's annexation of Scotland, receive his just deserts. There was no friendly face awaiting Wallace at any point on his journey. He was there to be humiliated as much as possible, both mentally and physically.

As the *Lanercost Chronicle* (Lanercost being a priory near the border with Scotland that Wallace had visited during his invasion of northern England) reported:

> *The vilest doom is fittest for thy crimes,*
> *Justice demands that thou should die three times,*
> *Thou pillager of many a sacred shrine,*
> *Butcher of thousands, threefold death be thine!*
> *So shall the English from you gain relief,*
> *Scotland! Be wise and choose a nobler chief.*

The same old story about the English being unable to understand why the Scots would follow Wallace is apparent in these lines. They saw their monarch as a shining light, the epitome of power and the mainstay of the feudal system. Wallace was nothing in their eyes. He was comparatively low born, and more important-ly, he put the welfare of Scotland and its people first. This they could not understand, when Scotland could and should be ruled by the magnanimous Edward i: why was Wallace not prepared to stand back and let his country be ruled from England? Is there any difference between the unseeing monks who compiled that chroni-cle in northern England – unseeing in the sense that they could not understand Wallace's patriotism, nor the viewpoint of the men who stood behind him at Stirling Bridge and Falkirk – and those in Scotland today who are happy with the Union, and happy with an English/Germanic monarchy that is able to call them 'subjects'?

First on the agenda of 'threefold death' for Wallace was the hanging. We do not know what his physical condition would have been like after the 19 day long journey south, not to mention the six mile ordeal he had suffered on his final journey. But I'm sure the executioners Edward had in his employment really knew their stuff, and they would have kept him in a reasonably lucid state. Perhaps a bucket of water would simply have been thrown over him to make sure he was suitably awake and aware of his sur-roundings. A tale has come down to us, perhaps an accurate one, that Wallace demanded to die with at least a little faith involved. He seems to have been a religious man, several accurate accounts having survived to provide us with proof of this. As he prepared to be hanged, Wallace is reported to have asked to have a Psalter held open before him, 'till they had done all that they wished to do with him.' If this were true, it would have at least been a focus for him, something to concentrate on whilst trying to blot out fear and to steel his soul to the ordeal ahead.

I have read of many London executions and the detail involved, but these accounts tend to be centred on ones that took place two and three hundred years after Wallace's time. I don't suppose the detail would have changed greatly though, as hideous torture and 'judicial' murder are torture and murder, no matter what. Minor details may have changed – for example, how they got Wallace into a position to actually hang him – but the outcome would have been the same. At Tyburn, for instance, a structure was created to replace the elm tree or trees originally used for hangings. The wooden structure comprised three uprights, with bars running between them. The 'triple tree' is how it became known, for the three horizontal beams running between the uprights made it triangular in fashion, and each beam could take several victims at once. But the court at Westminster Hall specifically sentenced that he should be conveyed to the 'Elms', so unless the name had stuck and was still used even though there was some kind of scaffold in place, he was actually to be hung from the branch of a tree. Hanging from trees rather than a scaffold was commonplace till comparatively recent times. As an example, several Scottish Jacobite prisoners were hung on the 'Capon Tree' in Brampton, east of Carlisle, in 1745–46.

In the later accounts I have read, many prisoners were conveyed to their place of execution in a cart, which was used as part of the process. They would simply be made to stand in the cart, their hands tied behind their backs, the noose draped over their heads, and the horse leading the cart would be made to trot forward a little, allowing the victim to dangle. It is then possible that this was the method used for Wallace. The hanging was only intended to throttle him, of course; he was to be kept alive for the spectacle ahead. So there would have to be some attention given to the length of the rope, as they would not want him to 'fall' or jerk suddenly, as that could break his neck prematurely and ruin the spectacle for the watching crowds.

One other vital point is that Wallace would probably have been stripped naked beforehand. A good hangman knew how to please his audience. Dextrous use of timing and technique during this slow strangulation and build up of blood pressure could not only result in the victim ridding himself of whatever was in his stomach, but also ensure that he would have an erection during the process. Very good hangmen were reported to be able to make their victims ejaculate, to the major cheering and applause of the crowd. But Wallace, jerking, kicking, would have been oblivious to the noise. The inability to breathe, the awful pain and pressure in his neck, the feeling that his head would explode from the constriction of his blood flow, would have been his major concerns. Trying to get a breath, trying to get a breath, his survival instincts making him struggle for even a gasp of air. The hangman would be timing all this very carefully, and when he decided that his victim was almost at the point of no return, with a wave of his hand he would have an accomplice either lower the rope or simply cut through it. In the later executions I have read of, the victim was then bodily manhandled onto the cart, which had been kept nearby. He would have been roughly thrown onto it, onto his back, ready for the disembowelling to begin. The victim would have been gasping for air, stunned and dazed, and still in incredible pain from the hanging finished only seconds before. Wallace would have been aware of what was happening, but would have been confused and probably in such distress that he was powerless to resist the down stroke of the blade.

In Scotland, we never went in much for such horrific sentences as disembowelling. The axe was the chosen means of dispatch for those accused of treason or being a traitor. Quick and clean. There was the odd burning, but that seemed to be the lot for those involved in religious crimes in some way, and was more around the time of the Reformation. Certainly, most people are aware that in France, Joan of Arc was burned at the stake for heresy. Burning seemed to be the chosen way to 'purify' where religion was concerned.

I have also seen it written that hanging, drawing and quartering was a punishment specifically thought up to dishonour Wallace. But that was certainly not the case, as it was not an unusual sentence, as is often thought, especially in London. I don't think it was so widespread in the English provinces, but in London it was almost an everyday occurrence. Tyburn eventually took over as the main place of execution in London, and Smithfield drifted into the background a little. This may come as a shock to many people – it certainly did to me when I discovered it – but the very lowest estimate for the amount of people who suffered this means of a slow death at Tyburn between the 1200s and 1783, the last year when such an end was recorded at that place of execution, is 50,000. And 100,000 people may be nearer the mark. An amount like that is just jaw dropping – all those poor souls who died in such agony. Some terrible eyewitness accounts survive. Children of nine and ten were disembowelled for theft. Can you imagine the terror those wee ones must have felt when their cell doors opened and they knew their last journey was about to begin? And crowds would flock to watch such spectacles. There were even 'boilings' at Smithfield. In one famous case a cook by the name of Rose was placed in a pot and boiled to death because he had cooked a meal for the Bishop of Rochester and two people who had eaten it died of food poisoning!

But there was one account that stuck in my mind when I read of it. One man, after being hung, was lifted bodily onto the cart for the disembowelling to begin. He was still reasonably conscious, and as the executioner lifted his blade, he somehow managed to summon up enough energy to sit up slightly and punch his tormentor. The executioner was not best pleased by this action, and, grabbing his victim by the throat and pushing him back, he made his disembowelling last for three quarters of an hour, delighting the crowd with his ability to keep his victim screaming in agony throughout. I try to imagine what this must have been like. I try to imagine the terror of those who were forced to undergo this inhumanity, how standing to receive the noose must have felt; and even to imagine the indescribable, the executioner making that belly cut and plunging his hands in to pull out your entrails, still steaming, for the delectation of those watching. And I think of Wallace. What pains me most is to think of the few seconds he had before the cut of the knife to his private parts. As a prelude to his disembowelling, Wallace was to have his genitalia removed, cut off and burnt. *Abscisis genitalibus* is how it is reported. Did he have a few seconds of flashback, to think of faces, of companions, of friends who had assisted in his campaigns? Did he get a chance to picture Scotland in his mind? Snow covered hills, or tree filled glens, or rushing rivers over rocks? And know that he would never see his country again? Or the face of the girl he loved? Then the knife would plunge in to his belly, and the agony would blot out every other feeling and emotion. Parts of his body being ripped out, but not bringing death. Praying for it to end. Having to endure the unendurable. That indescribable pain. Hoping that the blanket of death would cover him and end it all. How long it lasted we will never know. A fire, a brazier, burned nearby. As his intestines were pulled out, they were conveyed to the waiting flames and thrown upon them. The flames sparkling and crackling with their shrivelling, blackening fuel.

And once his stomach had been emptied, it was time to open his rib cage, and he would probably have been raised so that the cheering mob could see that his heart still beat within. With a roar from the crowd the executioner would have reached in and grabbed the heart of William Wallace in his hands. For a moment he held the still-living heart of a hero in his grasp. Then he gave a tug, and pulled the heart from its place, the ruptured arteries spouting blood. It is said there was just enough time for the executioner to show the heart to the victim before his eyes glazed. That he could see his heart giving its last few beats while held by another. Then Sir William Wallace, Guardian of Scotland, gave a last jerk, and was no more. He was oblivious to the chanting of the crowd. Onlookers would have scrambled forward to dip fragments of cloth into the spilt blood of the deceased. Lucky ones would have managed to grasp pieces of the clothing of which he had been divested. Superstition made these things lucky tokens, or they could be sold on to others as mementos. Strange to think that for several years afterwards, specimens of Wallace's blood would have done the rounds.

Then the organs would have been taken from the broken body. His heart, liver, kidneys and lungs were taken out one by one, held aloft as trophies, and then thrown onto the flames of the brazier. His lifeless body would then have been relegated to the axe man. He would have cut the head from the body in a mighty swipe. It would have been lifted to please the crowd, the dishonouring of the body of Wallace still continuing, before being tossed to the man whose duty it was to convey it to London Bridge. But Wallace no longer cared.

By the time these acts had taken place, he would have been nothing more than an empty carcass, like those one sometimes sees of a cow in a butcher's. Just the flesh and bones, the casing of a once proud body. Then the axe would rise and fall to chop the carcass into its respective quarters. The final disrespectful act. These were to be taken north and displayed, to warn the Scots of the might of England and what the penalty was to cross Edward Longshanks.

As mentioned before, the head was taken through the city to London Bridge. It was probably dipped in pitch, or perhaps even boiled first to ensure that it would not rot away too quickly or be picked clean by the scavenging birds. It was thrust onto a spike on the end of a long pole, and stuck out from the defensive tower on the drawbridge at an angle of forty-five degrees. Most old prints of London seem to show the view from the south, the Thames in the foreground and London Bridge running back to the city, St Paul's rising above the cluster of houses atop Ludgate Hill. On many of these prints if you look closely you can see the heads on their poles sticking out on the bridge. Visitors and dignitaries would approach the city from the south. They would look up at this macabre display. And for a while they looked up at the head of Wallace. The brain that loved his country and people shrivelled and gone. His sightless eyes oblivious to the coming and going of the river traffic below.

How long it was there we will never know. Was it eventually taken down, to be replaced with another, fresher example? Did a strong wind topple it, to fall to the pavement below? Or did it land with a splash in the Thames, and sink into its dark watery depths?

Perhaps it was taken down with others after a suitable time, and buried in some church's charnel house, but I doubt it, as to the English he was *persona non grata*.

His body having been quartered, the four parts were taken north. They were conveyed to Newcastle, Berwick, Stirling and Perth. It is recorded that the man responsible for conveying these body parts north was Sir John de Segrave, who received 10 shillings

– 50 pence in modern money – for his trouble. As a soldier only earned a penny or so per day, it was I suppose a reasonable sum to earn for the task. His instructions said that it was 'for the terror and rebuke to all who would pass by and behold them.' The man driving the cart that long road north could have leaned back and pulled aside the covering to expose all that remained of the body of Wallace.

Newcastle seems a strange choice. I can only assume that it was chosen because of Wallace's invasion of northern England after Stirling Bridge in the winter of 1297-8. He raided as far as the walls of Newcastle, and perhaps Edward wanted to display his power to the citizens by showing how he had prevailed over Wallace in the end. It was his right arm and the connected piece of body that were displayed here, hung above the bridge over the Tyne – 'over the common sewer.' Next stop was Berwick-upon-Tweed, where his right leg was pulled from the cart. There is a street in the town called Wallace Green, and the suggestion has been made that its name comes from its being the spot where the limb was displayed.

On, probably following the line of the old Roman road all the way to Stirling, the same road that a mighty army would follow from England nine years later, only to be annihilated at Bannockburn. The cart stopped at Stirling and Wallace's left arm was removed, raised up onto the shattered timbers of Stirling Bridge, still blackened and broken from Wallace's victory there in 1297, eight years before. It was nailed into place. This bridge was the main crossing point from northern Scotland into southern Scotland. The way that something like 80% of travellers would use. The River Forth was too wide east of there, although ferries plied it at various points, such as at Queensferry, where the Forth Bridges stand today. Further west were the wetlands of the Flanders Moss and the edge of the Highlands, and the paths known only to locals and men who wanted to keep a low profile. So many crossed the Forth at Stirling, either over the broken bridge or by an adjacent ferry, and looked up at the arm of William Wallace. On extremely dry summer days it is still possible to see the stumps of the old Stirling Bridge, just below the surface of the water – it stands several yards upstream from the stone Stirling Bridge that graces the site today. It was this very bridge that was the crux of the battle in 1297, and was where Wallace's arm was displayed.

It is confusing to think that people in Scotland would pass these body parts without trying to take them down and dispose of them in a chivalrous manner. Many of the members of the armies that had fought with Wallace must have looked at that arm on Stirling Bridge and remembered him well in life. But there is a legend that that arm was eventually taken by the monks from nearby Cambuskenneth Abbey, from which the Abbey Craig where the Wallace Monument stands took its name, and buried in the consecrated ground of their graveyard.

On to Perth, where Wallace's left leg was displayed, although there is no record of exactly where it was placed within the town. The *Lanercost Chronicle* mentioned that Aberdeen was a destination, rather than Perth, but I think the destinations in the court records in London are correct and that it is a mistake by the chronicler. That does not altogether curb the legend, however, that the star on the wall at the gateway at the back of St Machar's Cathedral in Aberdeen marks the burial place of one of Wallace's limbs. There does not seem to be any basis for this, but one never knows. Someone could have brought the part from Perth north surreptitiously!

So Wallace was gone. He had taken the risk, no questions asked, when England had invaded. He knew what the consequences would be if he should fail in his quest. But his great legacy was for the future. Stories of Wallace would be passed through the generations, through the centuries, and Wallace would become a talisman, a symbol, his name a byword for freedom. Edward Longshanks thought that by destroying Wallace in such a base manner he would go away, that the Scots would not think him worthy. But he had given us a martyr. The stories grew over the years, till Wallace, an ordinary man, took on the guise of a superman. And his shadow stands over Scotland still. And no matter the plans of Longshanks, we remember William Wallace.

CHAPTER EIGHT

The Walk Comes Together

I HAVE TRIED TO PORTRAY WALLACE'S last days in part by talking about what is on the ground today. It is obvious that Wallace still has an influence and effect on modern Scotland, not in a longing for the past, but in a longing for a time when Scotland was an independent state, a state that the memory of Wallace's fight epitomises.

When I wrote my book On the Trail of William Wallace in the 1990s, I mentioned that I would walk the route he was dragged through London on the 700th anniversary of the original day – Tuesday 23 August 2005. It seemed quite far distant, that date, when I wrote the book, but time passes and the 2000s came up with amazing speed! That simple statement in the book created quite a stir too. People of Scots blood from all over the planet contacted me, saying that they also wanted to be in London on the day. It was just their way of making a connection with Wallace. The more I thought about it, the more I began to think of Wallace, far from home and alone, facing his final ordeal. I wanted to put something together, a personal tribute.

At first I toyed with cycling to London. I've always been reasonably fit, and I thought I might just be able to pull that off in the same timescale, the 19 days from Wallace's capture at Robroyston on the third of August, to his appearance in London on the twenty-second, before his trial on the twenty-third. Wallace would most probably have been tied to a horse on his journey, so cycling the route in the same timescale seemed fair enough. But that idea was soon scuppered when I mentioned it to members of the Society of William Wallace. Christine MacLeod, who is currently the top lady at the Weaver's Cottage, a National Trust for Scotland property in Kilbarchan, said, 'You really need to walk it.' She was right, but I knew it would be murder trying to walk 400 plus miles in 19 days.

At the end of the day, though, my mind went back to Wallace and all he had to undergo, and I knew I had to at least give it a go.

So I started walking. I was really pretty rubbish at it, although I had always worked out in the gym. I was used to motorcycles and cars, and even a few miles were an effort, but I pushed on and hoped that I could inure myself to walking many miles. First time I walked four miles I was pleased with myself! But I soldiered on. I remember the first time I walked from my home in East Kilbride into Glasgow, some 10 miles – then I got the train home. I was sore for a day or two, but impressed with my own efforts. About this time I started to tell folk that I intended to try and walk from Glasgow to London in 19 days. That got some strange reactions. There did not seem to be a middle ground. People either said, 'I could walk to London no bother', or, '400 to 450 miles in 19 days, you must be stark raving mad!'

The biggest problem to surmount is the fact that I am still 19 inside my own head. The aches and pains kept telling me that I was not, but I had the knowledge of all that Wallace had to undergo to push me on. I tried running on treadmills and went to various fitness classes to help push my fitness levels, but I found that the only real way to train for a long walk was to... well... walk.

I started to get a severe pain in my right heel (I'm left handed, so left footed too, thus it was not because I favoured that side) that got so bad I had to see a foot specialist. I explained to him that when I first got out of bed in the morning I could not take my weight on my right foot, and would end up on the floor. After struggling for fifteen minutes I would eventually be able to put my weight on both feet.

It turns out I had *plantar fasciitis* – a condition where the large tendon that runs along the inner underside of the foot, forming the arch of the foot, comes away from the heel. It is attached like fingers to the heel and runs right up to the toes, and when it tears away... well, you can imagine the pain. When you are in bed at night with your foot relaxed, it partially heals. So when I was rising in the morning and putting my weight on it, it came away again – hence the falling down. After a few consultations it was decided that the best course of action would be a cortisone injection into my heel. The doctor told me it might not cure the problem, but would help to hide it, and I would have tried anything to help me complete the now-intended walk.

The nurse did say to me, as an aside, that she 'would rather go through childbirth than get an injection like that in the heel.' This worried me a little, as I had never heard a woman make such a statement, but how bad could an injection be? When I went for the actual jab, the doctor told the attendant nurse to fill me with painkiller before he came back to inject. She gave me several painkilling injections in the heel, whilst saying, 'Are you sure you need this done? Getting cortisone injected into the heel is agony.' How sore could it be after the painkillers? I also remembered again what Wallace went through and figured I could handle this. Then the doc injected me. It probably only lasted about 15-20 seconds. My whole body arched with the agony of it. I started to convulse and was still in the arched position when I remember the doctor telling me that he had actually finished and I could relax now. But I was stuck in that position from the shock of it! Two hours later I was still shaking from the memory of the pain. The foot felt a different shape afterwards and it was sore for several weeks, but it settled down eventually and I could train hard again.

Not long after this, early in 2003, I was in London with my daughter Kimberley and I walked the route that Wallace was dragged through London for the first time. I wanted to wait till the 700th anniversary in 2005, but I felt that if others wanted to do it too, I had best familiarise myself with the street layout. As I set out my foot started to swell and the pain was extraordinary. I managed to complete the route, but later in my room when I took my shoe off, my right foot was like a rubber glove blown up like a balloon, with the toes looking for all the world like the stubby fingers protruding from the end. I could not even bear to have a sheet over it. The next morning it was a struggle to get to Euston for the train back north. I had to hop to the taxi leaning on my daughter.

I thought I had a stress fracture brought on by the constant walking, especially as friends warned me that such a thing might happen. But on the journey north the swelling went down and by the time the train arrived in Scotland I could stand on it again. I was nonplussed. What the hell had caused this? Bobby Bishop, one of the guys in the gym where I train, is a chiropodist, and when I told him the story, he took a look at my foot. 'Gout', he said. 'What?' says I. 'You have gout', he replied. 'That's what that redness is at the base of the big toe on your right foot.' Now, I know from recent medical evidence that gout is caused by beer drinking, and I do like the odd drink, but not to excess. In fact, far less is imbibed by me than is taken in by most of my mates as standard. I went to my doctor, and he immediately said 'gout' too, so that was that. Gout is actually caused by a build up of uric acid in your body, which gathers in your extremities and forms as crystals in your joints. In my case it was at the base of the big toe in my right foot. The crystals are very sharp, and it is this irritation which causes the pain. For this I was prescribed Allopurinol, which I'll probably be on for the rest of my days, and it made me incredibly ill. Took me ages to get used to it. But it was worth it if it meant I could get back to training.

Forward to September 2003, and I was in the gym training with Davie White. Davie is retired, but is incredibly fit and strong, and he pushed me to extremes in my training, knowing that I had the walk to do. Suddenly I began to feel strange. He asked me what was wrong. I told him that when I stood still I felt okay, but as soon as I moved or exerted myself, I felt 'trippy' and there was an unreality about everything. So I ended up going to Hairmyres Hospital in East Kilbride, where they connected me to a machine to check my heart. Suddenly all hell broke loose, and I had a dozen people working on me. I was at rest yet my heart was going at almost 300 beats per minute! I was in hospital for several days, drugged up to get my heart back on track. It turns out that this was just the start. Over the next few months my heart was all over the place. So much so that I got taken in for a heart operation in May 2004. In through the main artery in my thigh, so at least the nice pectorals I had built up during training never got severed. I just had to keep telling myself that if Wallace could go through all that took place in his final couple of hours, I could surely take this punishment to try and deliver some sort of tribute to him.

The best part of the operation was that I was conscious throughout. It was quite strange to lie there with someone working inside my heart through my thigh. Scared beforehand? You bet I was. The first operation didn't work, but I did my best to take the myriad medicines and continue training. I got my second operation in April 2005, not too long before the walk was meant to commence. This time I was on the table four and a half hours. It took several weeks for there to be an appreciable difference, but it did eventually settle my heart down from its erratic wanderings.

I stepped up the walking. Did a few 30-mile-plus days to push myself to the limit. There were constant setbacks. It was almost as if someone up there was saying, 'It was unbearable torture that Wallace had to undergo. We'll give you a bit of pain so that you realise in the very depth of your soul what this man suffered in the name of Scotland.' And I do. Like Wallace, all I want to see is my country free. I was 47 when I did the walk. Wallace was probably only in his early 30s when he was butchered. I am deeply humbled. I have been given these extra years to look around me at the country of my birth. So many times I have walked across the battlefields where Wallace once walked, and I am lucky that 700 years on I am able to visit the spots where the great and the good once were.

But Scots are Scots. When I made it public that the walk would take place, I was actually called a 'glory seeker' by some. Jeez. I wish some of these people would go out and just walk 10 miles and feel the pain. Do they think I really wanted to walk 25 miles a day for nearly three weeks? And I underwent a lot of pain to make the attempt. But I never expected or wanted it to be easy.

When deciding what to wear while undertaking such a walk, or even to practise walking, it was all trial and error. The stuff that worked for me I sussed out myself. I had tried surfing the net to see if I could find any information on any famous round-the-world walkers or similar, but did not find any details on what to wear. For me it is a pair of Nike Shox training shoes, bought one size too big. I lace them up tight so they don't slip, but the extra room seems to

ensure there is no rubbing so I don't really blister. I can go through
the soles of a pair in 200 miles though, and they are not cheap (I
am Scottish after all!). I know this will not be the answer for everyone who wants to walk long distances, but I've written it down as
I could not find these details anywhere else.

A decent waterproof lightweight jacket is a must. But you do
need to spend good money to get something breathable. I have a
Gore-Tex one – just a skin, no lining, as the amount of heat you
generate walking is surprising. Some days I would start cold, and
after a couple of miles I would be bare-chested, running with
sweat, even when the weather was not too good. I could see folk
driving past, saying to themselves, 'Look at that nutter!' Even in
winter I would just wear a t-shirt, although if it were really cold I
would wear a long sleeved one under my jacket. And I always had
gloves and a hat in my pockets.

I wondered if I was sweating so much because I was unfit, but
one of the older guys in the gym was a marathon runner in his
younger days and still walked something like eight miles every
other day. I asked him if he could build up enough heat walking to
get a sweat going. He replied, 'First thing I do when I get into the
house, son, is throw my semmit and drawers into the washing
machine.' Well, that answered that, then! I found that wearing
heavy socks caused rubbing, so I would just wear light M&S cotton
socks, mainly because of their comfort value.

The one thing that you definitely need is Vaseline. And buy a
lot of it! A good dollop on your nether regions to stop chafing is
most important. They can get rubbed red raw and if this happens
you will not be able to walk for days. No use if you have a walk
like mine to make, where there is a time scale and you have to walk
day after day. Also, a light coating on the parts of your feet likely
to blister is a good preventative measure.

I know all the country lanes and paths near where I live as I
walked them when I was younger, and motorcycled them in more
recent years. I walked many of them again when I started training,
but it gets boring walking familiar territory. So I started driving to
railway stations and walking to distant stations on the same line so

that I could get a train back to where I had parked. I walked routes that I had always wanted to see. The Forth and Clyde Canal, for instance. Canal towpaths can be a delight to walk. They are generally level and there are ducks and swans galore. You get to see familiar landscapes from different angles too. I love Scotland with my heart and soul, and just watching the hills slowly roll by as you amble along, especially when you get fitter, is marvellous. One worrying aspect was 'mooing' at cows and 'baaing' at sheep. Not consciously, of course. I would walk past cows on lonely roads and find myself 'mooing' at them. Whole herds would stop grazing to look at me in that mid-munch disgusted manner that only cows can do.

Finding things was another plus. Interesting buildings and memorials; there are a hundred places I can think of where I just paused while training to look at something of real beauty. But most important of all was the enrichment of my life. I got to understand Scotland a little better; her topography, her landscape. And a little more of her history, like when I walked the aforementioned canal and realised that every inch of that astonishing feat of engineering was built with shovels, picks and wheelbarrows. And sweat. How the Forth and Clyde follows the line of the Roman Antonine Wall that Scotland wears like a belt across her slender waist. How more than a millennium and a half before the construction of the canal the Romans had discovered that line of least resistance that is so obvious in the walking of its length.

I walked the length of the Union Canal too, and the first few miles from the Falkirk Wheel were great. I walked across the base of the battlefield where Bonnie Prince Charlie won the second Battle of Falkirk in 1746. Then, a few miles on I crossed right across the site of Wallace's battle of 1298. Looking across to Woodend Farm and the slope where the schiltroms stood, I realised that I was probably right on the spot from which Longshanks stared across at the mighty figure of Wallace exhorting his men to do their best for Scotland. I couldn't help but stop for a moment and try to imagine that day.

But I also grew to understand the world I read and wrote

about, the world of medieval Scotland. How it must have felt to have been an ordinary foot soldier at the time of Wallace and Bruce. Your average person can walk about four miles in an hour, and I am no exception. It has been reported that Roman troops could cover 20 miles in five hours' marching, but that is especially impressive when you think of the armour they wore and the weapons they carried. I thought of the many English armies of invasion, and how they would muster at Newcastle to take the east coast route into Scotland, and how just simple walking would have taken up most of their daily existence.

And I was able to think of Wallace himself, covering Scotland in all weathers, most likely having to sleep rough much of the time. We may live in a technological age, but the lie of the land and the shape of the hills are just as he saw them, and I would look out at the Ochils or the Campsies and see them very much as he did, seven centuries before.

What always surprised me was the distance one can cover in a day. Journeys between one town and another that I imagined would take a couple of days to walk originally, I found I could cover in one long day. I hoped that eschewing motor transport was giving me an insight into what life was like for Wallace. Walking point to point through a country under foreign occupation, taking little known routes, would have been much of his lot. Unconsciously I had adopted some of the lifestyle he was used to, to commemorate him in some way. I intended to follow in his footsteps in walking to London; I probably walked in them during some of my training. And I got to see a little of Scotland as he saw it.

But I also learned how soft we have become. I thought of Bonnie Prince Charlie's army gathering at Glenfinnan, walking to Derby, before retiring all the way north again to the massacre at Culloden. They carried all their weaponry on their backs, and did not have our modern fabrics or footwear. For thousands of years our ancestors marched. Marched to follow the herds north as the last Ice Age retreated. Marched to counter the aggressive inroads of the Roman invaders, or to invade England, or to counteract armies spilling north over the Border. They even walked their way to the immigrant ships when the land was cleared after the collapse of the clan system. And it did not stop there. Many walked their way to their new homes over the continents of the New World. Lucky were those who had the means to use a horse, and I hope Wallace did so on the long pilgrimage he made to Rome on Scotland's behalf! And I worried about walking to London?

CHAPTER NINE

Creating the Commemoration

SO I DECIDED THAT I would walk to London. A personal pilgrimage, but it was also a catalyst to try and raise awareness that 2005 was the 700th anniversary of the murder of the hero of Scotland. I hoped that if the press picked up on it, it would ensure that the public of Scotland knew too. Otherwise I could see 23 August 2005 come and go without a mention.

I wanted to organise some sort of commemoration in London, so my mind started to go down that road. I remembered the Butchers' Company in London had contacted the Society of William Wallace several years previously, asking if we would be interested in doing something, like having a stall at Smithfield, as they were trying to kick-start a resurgence in the St Bartholomew's Fair. Not on its original medieval scale of course, but with funfairs and the like. They had contacted us purely because of the Smithfield connection, as Wallace had been executed there, but I'm sure that they did not realise that Wallace's death was most likely the opening spectacle for the fair in 1305.

I did not really see how we could get involved at the time, but it gave me an opening to try and start something for 2005. I duly contacted the Butcher's Company, who are one of the guilds of tradesmen of London, an old and auspicious company, and asked about their plans for 2005 and whether the Society of William Wallace could get involved. Unfortunately they had no plans to put on a fair in the 700th anniversary year, so I had run down a blind alley. I would have liked them to have been involved. There would have been an unintentional irony there somewhere, the Butchers' Company of Smithfield running St Bartholomew's Fair, and helping out with a commemoration of Wallace! I did make enquiries regarding the guild premises at Smithfield, as there is a hall there that holds a couple of hundred people. 'No problem', was the reply. 'We can do it for £2,500, but you have to use our caterers on top of that' (which at the most basic rate was something like £10 – £15 for a finger buffet per person!) And music was not allowed, so that was that. What seemed to be the usual rates in London were astronomical compared to Scottish charges. Most places up here, if you guarantee them a crowd, are happy to supply the premises, knowing they will make money at the bar!

Then I thought of the last thing that Wallace saw. I know it may have meant nothing to him in his extremity, but it was there when he was, and it was reflected in his darkening eyes. The church of St Bartholomew the Great, the oldest church in London. The church from which St Bartholomew's Fair took its name. I had been inside it before of course, because of its location, its proximity to Wallace's end, with the plaque to his memory only a few feet away from its porch entrance. It is a stunning building inside – not large, but high-roofed and narrow-naved. Its ancient age hangs heavy on the air within. After Westminster Abbey it is probably the most historic church in London, though it does not attract the visitor numbers of that venerable pile. In fact, you can sometimes find yourself alone in St Bart's. I made a few tentative enquiries to the church. Yes, they were willing to discuss holding a service commemorating Sir William Wallace. I was elated. It was the right place. It meant I could look for eminent speakers and did not have to worry about public address systems and the like. But I also knew the hard work was only just beginning.

Things fell into place from St Bart's onward, and I knew that some things were meant to be. Divine providence began to take over. When things are right, they just work – and they were, and did. If I were to have a church service, I would need a churchman to hold it all together. I got in touch with an old friend, whom I had actually met through a recommendation from that late great Scottish author, Nigel Tranter. The Rev Alan Sorensen was someone I had a common interest with. He was passionate about Scottish castles and tower houses. I tracked him down, as he had moved to Greenock to take over a parish there. He was very interested in presiding over a service of commemoration for William Wallace, even though it was to be in London, and when I offered him expenses he would not hear of it. Again and again people pulled their weight, no questions asked. The fact that this was about Wallace and Scotland was payment enough.

It was around this time that I had an idea that had many looking at me as if I had two heads. I attended the Battle of Sheriffmuir commemoration in 2002, which took place in the now sadly defunct Sword Hotel, which sat immediately below the National Wallace Monument. At night, sitting in the glass conservatory-like extension, I looked up at the floodlit Wallace Monument sitting on the Abbey Craig above. This made me think. At the following Stirling Bridge commemoration in September 2003, I said to the guys, 'I want to have a coffin in the church in London, something we can bring back to Scotland and bury.' I think they all thought I had really lost it this time. But there was a strange reasoning in my mind where this was concerned, and I explained: 'Wallace was torn to bits alone and far from home. Longshanks did this so we would forget him, forget the fight for Scotland's freedom. But we have never forgotten him, though his atoms were scattered to the four winds. Where does he live now?' One or two thought about it and pointed to their hearts and heads. 'Exactly', I said. 'He lives within our hearts and minds. If we have a coffin in the church that we can fill with messages containing our thoughts, then if he lives within the Scottish people it is like gathering his spirit if we write it all down.'

It took a while for it to sink in, but some could see what I was getting at. 'Where would we bury this coffin?' one or two asked. I replied that it could be anywhere in Scotland, as surely someone would be happy to let us have a bit of land to bury the 'spirit of Wallace.'

Now, I need to point out something here. I don't seriously believe that I was bringing Wallace back or burying his spirit forever. Wallace will always be there, will always live as long as Scots crave the freedom for their nation that each generation recognises. I just wanted to show that seven hundred years on we have not for-

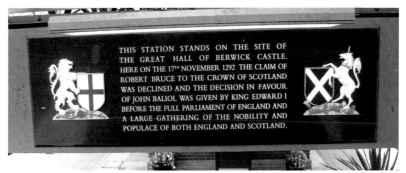

The plaque above the platforms at Berwick-upon-Tweed railway station that marks where John Balliol was chosen to be King of Scots in 1296. (DRR)

Wallace's biographer, Blind Harry, tells us that Menteith agreed to betray Wallace to the English in the church at Rutherglen. (DRR)

A little known and generally unnoticed memorial plaque to Wallace's betrayal on the wall of Rutherglen's Mitchell Arcade. (DRR)

Wallace's Well, near the monument to his capture at Robroyston. Probably the spot where he had his last drink as a free man. (DRR)

The monument at Robroyston that marks the site of the farm where Wallace was captured. It was raised by public subscription and unveiled in 1900. (DRR)

Westminster Hall, the oldest part of the Houses of Parliament. It was in this building that the sham trial of Wallace took place. (DRR)

The view to Westminster Abbey from just outside Westminster Hall. Longshanks was buried within in 1307. This is the view from the place where Wallace's dragging through the streets began. (DRR)

Bust of Charles I marking the place of his execution. It is above the door of the Banqueting House in Whitehall. Wallace passed this spot on the first leg of his final journey. (DRR)

The 'Eleanor Cross' that gave Charing Cross its name. These were erected by Longshanks to mark the spots where his late wife's coffin rested. The original stood here when Wallace was dragged past. (DRR)

The church of St Mary's le Strand. Here Bonnie Prince Charlie converted to the Anglican faith, yet another Scottish connection on the route of Wallace's last journey. (DRR)

Just after St Mary's, Essex Street runs off to the right. This plaque marks the spot where Prince Charlie is said to have stayed on his secret visit to London in the years after Culloden. (DRR)

The Temple Bar outside the High Courts of Justice. It marks the site of a Templar toll barrier that was here in 1305. (DRR)

'Mary Queen of Scots' house'. It has a life-sized statue of Mary on its front. Mary never actually stayed in, or visited London while she was alive! She is buried in Westminster Abbey. (DRR)

Plaque that marks where the scaffold stood on Tower Hill. Scottish Jacobites were executed here. (DRR)

Looking up Ludgate Hill towards St Paul's Cathedral. This was Wallace's route up towards the original church, which was destroyed in the Great Fire of London in 1666. (DRR)

Greyfriar's Church. Here was buried the Queen of Edward II of England. Strange that Wallace was taken by the spot where his lover from *Braveheart* was to be buried, and the two would be linked in a film 690 years later! (DRR)

The Tower of London from Tower Hill. Wallace was meant to be kept in the Tower but the crowds were too great. He passed it on his last journey. (DRR)

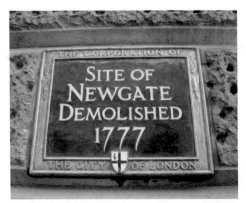

Plaque marking the site of the 'New Gate'. Wallace was taken through this gate on his way out of the City to the Smithfield. (DRR)

The plaque, erected by patriots in the 1950s, on the side wall of St Bartholomew's Hospital, that marks the vicinity where Wallace was horribly executed. (DRR)

The church of St Bartholomew the Great, the oldest church in London. It was probably the last thing that Wallace saw. (DRR)

The rear view of the church of St Bartholomew the Great. Other buildings today hem in the church and it is difficult to get a good overall view. (DRR)

The imposing and ancient interior of St Bartholomew the Great, where the memorial service to Wallace was held on the 700th anniversary of his murder. (DRR)

The tomb of Rahere, the founder of St Bartholomew the Great. When the tomb was opened his skeleton was still wearing his leather monk's sandals! (DRR)

Looking down the old entrance pathway to London Bridge. The church is St Magnus the Martyr, which contains a model of the old bridge.(DRR)

Plaque marking the approach to London Bridge on the church of St Magnus the Martyr. Wallace's head passed by here on its way from Smithfield, to be 'spiked' on the bridge itself. (DRR)

View downstream to Tower Bridge from the current London Bridge. The London Bridge where Wallace's head was 'spiked' was just a few yards downstream from this one. (DRR)

A Saltire in the sky above London, 5:45am on 23 August 2005.
(Nick Brand)

A 75 foot Saltire hung from London Bridge early in the morning of 24 August 2005 by members of the SNP and *Siol nan Gaidheal*. (Bruce Ogilvie)

David Ross in Westminster Hall on 23 August, with SNP MP Angus
Brendan MacNeil. (Eddie Tait)

The plaque in Westminster Hall, 23 August 2005. (walkforwallace.com)

The 'Spirit of Wallace' in the side chapel of St Bartholomew the Great. (Nick Brand)

The 'Spirit of Wallace' in the church. (Jim Gee)

The procession to the London Welsh Centre. (Jim Crawford)

The procession continues (GHM)

The Alaskan Highlanders outside the London Welsh Centre. (Nick Brand)

David with Ronnie Browne of the Corries in the London Welsh Centre.
(Scott Harvie)

Dancing to *Clann an Drumma* in the hall. (Eddie Tait)

More dancing in the hall (Eddie Tait)

David with Duncan Fenton, of the Society of William Wallace, in the London Welsh Centre. (walkforwallace.com)

The 'Spirit of Wallace' in the Stirling Smith Art Gallery and Museum, Stirling, 25 August 2005. (walkforwallace.com)

David leads out the coffin from the Stirling Smith Art Gallery and Museum, 10 September 2005. (GHM)

Quilt commemorating David's Walk for Wallace made by Armadale Primary School, Primary 7 Class 2003-2004 and teacher Audra McKee.
(Audra McKee)

gotten, and though it has taken this long, we recognise and we remember. As an acquaintance commented, 'It is like a closure, the mourning that Wallace never had.'

As I explained all this, more and more people came on board. And as you can probably imagine, when I appraised St Bart's church of my plans they were wary to say the least. But I knew I had chosen wisely in the Rev Sorensen when he said that he would happily travel to London to chat with the rector at St Bart's, Dr Dudley, to assure him our aim was true. He was as good as his word, and did his best to allay any fears. There was no hidden agenda. I only wanted to do my best to honour a hero of Scotland. I know that there is irony in holding a commemoration in London on the spot where Wallace breathed his last. But that is just the way of it. I am a Scot, I want to see my country free, but if Wallace had been butchered anywhere else, then I would have held such a service there.

But there is one underlying undercurrent that I should touch on. Wallace really means something deep in the psyche of Scots. I honestly believe that he is perceived in a way that most national heroes are not. Perhaps because his fight is still relevant today, as we are, just as we were in his time, ruled from somewhere else and told we should be grateful. Wallace had to fight against the ruling classes of Scotland in his day, and many of our politicians today, aided by an England-based media, tell us that we should be grateful, be happy with Union. But it is all propaganda. I see through it as Wallace did.

So he is embedded in our souls. He really means something that, with all due respect, King Harold (of 1066 fame) and Nelson do not in England. And I knew that St Bart's would not really realise what Wallace means in our souls, or what this service would mean to those Scots attending. This would not just be a commemoration service. This would be at the heart and soul of what it means to be Scottish, in the true spirit of the word.

I knew money was going to be important. All the plans starting to form in my mind were going to cost money. I knew I would be digging deep into my own pocket because it was all so important to me, but it could also spiral beyond my means.

The bulk of Wallace monuments were raised by public subscription in the 19th and early 20th centuries. The memory of
Wallace is still strong and people dug deep to help. Jim Scott, a
mate from Perth who runs a wee patriot group in that locale, was
the first to turn up with a few cheques from people wanting to
help. Nick Brand, the head man from *Siol nan Gaidheal* (the Seed
of the Gael), a cultural and fraternal organisation dedicated to
looking after the well-being of Scotland, is a bit of a computer
whiz, and he set up the website www.walkforwallace.com to help
spread the word. There was a place on the site to pledge money,
and people did. I want them to know it all helped. Members of the
Society of William Wallace pledged money; members of the Tartan
Army, the Scottish national football team supporters, helped too. I
received a cheque from the *Guarde Ecosse*, Prince Michael of
Albany's personal guard. My friend Hugh Robertson got several
battle re-enactment groups together, and they staged a fight at
Dean Castle in Kilmarnock. This raised quite a bit of money and
they kindly donated it toward the Walk funds. But above all, I have
to mention a class from Armadale Primary School. They were the
2003/4 Primary Seven class, and in a couple of weeks they raised
£350! Nobody else came close. They had a sponsored walk, they
did some baking to sell to the other kids, they did all sorts. Their
teacher, Audra McKee, is a member of the Society of William
Wallace. Like all Scottish kids, they were enthralled by the stories
of Wallace and the other heroes of the Scottish Wars of
Independence. But there is a dark side to this. Audra was berated
by her 'superiors' for instilling a Scottishness in her kids. Is there
any other nation on the planet where a teacher can be frowned
upon for teaching children about where they came from, and for
giving them a pride in their country?

I turned up at the school to do a slide show and talk to the kids
about Wallace. As a surprise, they presented me with a tartan bag
with the £350 in it, and as I looked at all those untainted eager
faces, the tears started to flow. Can you imagine if every school in
Scotland instilled patriotism into the children? This is not about

brainwashing. Unionism has that cornered. It is about teaching children their past. The blood that stood behind Wallace at Stirling Bridge or behind Bruce at Bannockburn has not gone anywhere. It runs in the veins of the population of Scotland. Somewhat suppressed, but it is there still. A self-pride, a self-respect taught in our schools where Scotland is concerned is what is needed. It is about looking after your fellow Scots and the well being of our landscape. Litter is a huge problem in Scotland, and that is down to a lack of pride. Audra used to tell her kids that if they cared about and loved Scotland, they would not drop their sweetie papers and the like. The kids understood and took this on board. Her superiors may have frowned, but I'm sure Wallace would have approved.

I asked if this class could possibly come and attend the launch of my book *Desire Lines* at Elderslie Village Hall in May 2004. They took the stage and each kid stepped forward to say how they felt about Scotland, and kids have not been tainted by the propaganda inherent in Scottish society, and they tell it like it is. Their honesty, their simple love for their native heath had many an eye filling up.

They had a t-shirt designing competition too, and Fraser Keast won it and presented me with his winning 'Walk for Wallace' t-shirt. I promised him I would wear it as I actually crossed the Border. Just a simple thing, yet it meant so much to that boy. But it meant much to me too, that kids would care enough to work as hard as they did towards making a Wallace commemoration a success. I want them to know that their money went towards the costs of hiring St Bart's to hold the service. Every penny they raised helped to ensure that I could use the oldest church in London, the last thing Wallace saw. They made their own connection with Wallace. The great warrior and a class of school kids, born seven centuries apart, but both knew what being Scottish meant. I hope that they all grow to teach their own children that there is no shame in being Scottish and that the right to decide the destiny of your own is a right we should all have.

With the hall in place, I needed a coffin to carry the 'Spirit of Wallace.' My friend Hazel Eunson knew Kenny Fleming, who worked for the Co-operative Funeral Service, so she gave him a call. It must have been a strange conversation, with Hazel asking, 'Would it be possible to buy a large coffin?' and Kenny replying, 'Who for?' When the situation was explained, Kenny said that the Co-op would be happy to give us a coffin. Free. This was not the first time that someone would not take money as the recipient was Wallace, and Scotland, and it turned out to be far from the last.

As I had the church and the coffin in place, and the walk to London was up to me, I needed to look for somewhere to hold the evening event. Another piece of the jigsaw fell into place when I spoke to Sheila MacLean. Sheila is a member of the Society of William Wallace, an ex-pat who lives in London, and she asked if there was anything she could do to help as she knew the lay of the land down there pretty well. Sheila proved to be invaluable. Again and again the real patriotic help came from the womenfolk of Scotland. They know where their hearts lie and have an unquestioning loyalty and patriotism that some of the menfolk lack. Sheila suggested the Welsh Centre in Grays Inn Road as a suitable venue. She had attended ceilidhs there and thought it fitted the bill. As the name Wallace is really old Scots for 'Welshman', and it is thought that the Wallace family came north from the village of Ness on the Welsh Marches, there was something fitting in using the place. (They asked only reasonable money for hiring, too). When I explained to the Welsh lady who did the bookings why I was looking to hire the place, she asked about men in kilts, and when I told her that the bulk of the menfolk attending would be in kilts, it was a done deal! It was the perfect venue, as it held about the same number of people as the church did, and was only a mile away from Smithfield. Sheila also acted as a go between with St Bart's, which was handy. Amongst other things, she sorted out an organist for the service and brought the London Gaelic Choir on board, which was brilliant.

I was lucky enough to do an event in Perth with a great musician called Ted Christopher. As I play the guitar and have done a lot of songwriting in the past, I could admire Ted's ability to write songs with great feeling and pathos. He is from the Stirling area, and when the horror of the Dunblane massacre took place, when all those little children were gunned down at school, Ted wrote the tribute song that went to No. 1. Ted wanted to get involved with what I was doing in London and he was a brilliant addition to the project. He agreed to play the evening event with his fellow musicians, the Bannockburn Band. But he also wrote a song especially for the 700th anniversary. When he had it finished he phoned me and asked me to go out to his place near Braco. I'll never forget hearing the song for the first time. It was entitled 'I'm Coming Home':

I did not close my eyes for the last time,
Under Caledonian skies
With my good friends gathered all around me,
To say their last goodbyes,
But I will not be forgotten, in the heart of every Scot I still live on,
And it's time to fly the Saltire high –
My spirit's coming home.

Chorus

I'm coming home, back where I belong
It's coming home – my spirit's coming home
To Scotland, St Andrew and Freedom.

They tore apart my body so I could not rise on Judgement Day
But what they did not realise is now I'll never go away
Coming back to the land I love –
To the people I hold dear
To Scotland, St Andrew and Freedom.

Chorus

Returning after all this time
To Caledonia's skies,
To the country that I died for

So that our nation could survive
Once again to stand beside
The people I hold dear,
For Scotland, St Andrew and Freedom.

It was agreed that Ted would sing the song in St Bart's as part of the service, and I knew that with his incredible gutsy Scottish voice he would knock people dead. I reckoned there would not be a dry eye in the place, and I was glad I wasn't singing it as I knew I would have broken down halfway through! Ted recorded a couple of copies onto CD for me, and I played it to the odd patriotic friend in the car. Everyone was blown away and I think (strange as it may seem) the best comment was: 'I always said that I would have 'Caledonia' by Dougie MacLean played at my funeral, but that song by Ted has deposed it.'

I had always been a fan of *Clann an Drumma* (Children of the Drum), whose brand of Scottish music is blood stirring and almost primeval. They look like they have stepped out of late medieval Scotland in their tartans and leather. The band comprises several drummers and a piper. They are the way musicians would have been in the glens, with their thunderous loose style, unlike most pipe bands today whose roots lie in the strict discipline of the Scottish Army regiments. *Clann an Drumma* were busy touring in North America but promised to make time to return and play – first at the North East Wallace gathering in Aberdeen and Stonehaven, which takes place every year, then in London as part of the commemorations there.

Next musical coup was Ronnie Browne, one half of the legendary Corries. His partner in that almost mythical duo, Roy, tragically died of cancer too young. Too young to see Scotland get a parliament of sorts again. The Corries, of course, are famous the world over. Every ex-pat Scot, or person of Scottish descent in the New World, seems to have at least a couple of their CDs. I asked if Ronnie would sing 'Flower of Scotland' in the church. It is an oft-played song, but there is a huge difference between someone singing 'Flower of Scotland' and Ronnie Browne singing it.

I needed speakers too, but where to start? Like so much of the detail for the service, it all just started to fall into place. Alex Salmond, leader of the Scottish National Party, agreed. I am an admirer of Alex, and had been lucky enough to speak at dinners and the like alongside him in the past. I knew he would be able to speak with passion and aplomb on the day, and at least let the spirit of Wallace know that some of us are still carrying the torch in Scotland.

I was sitting eating my 'tea' (as we say about the evening meal in Scotland) one night when the phone rang. It was Sir Sean Connery. He wanted to come to the service, and I asked if he would say a few words. He said he would do everything he could to get there, but had contractual obligations and that I should not confirm him till he saw what he could do. I really hoped he would be able to make it. He is the most famous Scotsman on Earth, so I could not really ask for better to say a few words on the memory of Wallace, whose spirit touches us all. I was not going to advertise any of the 'names' attending in advance anyway. This commemoration was about Wallace, and that was understood right across the board. Nothing was to detract from this day that was especially for him. Unfortunately, just before I wrote this, Sean phoned to say he could not get away from what he was scheduled to do, but he did leave me with words of encouragement and told me that he supported all that I was doing.

Christine McLeod, the girl who had talked me into walking to London instead of letting me give myself an easier option, made something for me that I will treasure till the end of my days. As I said before, she works at the Weaver's Cottage in Kilbarchan, and she knows a lot about natural dyes and the like. She made me a plaid to wear for the 700th anniversary. Just in case you don't know, the plaid is the original Scottish garb from which the kilt is descended. It is a large rectangle of cloth, which you pleat and belt, and it can be worn in various ways to suit temperature and weather conditions. I often wore the plaid, but Christine's is very special, and I'd like to explain why.

When I was in my late teens, I read a book by that fabulous

descriptive writer H.V. Morton, entitled *In Scotland Again*, a follow up to his huge seller *In Search of Scotland*. His books were published in the 1920s and 30s, and he drove around on what were very empty roads by our standards, visiting people and places, and wrote about them with a candid charm. He had quite a large effect on me, and I have to admit that my book *Desire Lines* owes a great debt to his influence. *In Scotland Again* has him visit weavers in Kilbarchan, and I vividly remember reading the part about Willie Meikle, one of the great weavers, and one of the last of a dying breed.

Anyway, Christine has managed to gather knowledge of the old ways as much as humanly possible, and using old techniques she began work on my plaid. She teased the wool; she gathered plants, bark and moss from places associated with Wallace to create the dyes; she wove me a plaid in which the sett – the repeated patterns of lines that create tartan – was a representation of Wallace's life. For instance, there are 700 strands of russet, to mark each of the years since Wallace walked among us, and all of the colours and the number of strands have a special significance. There is even a green stripe that marks my daughter's age, representing new life. Christine has her own strands in there too. It is her way of being part of it all, of forging her own wee connection with Wallace.

And the twist? She wove the plaid by hand on her favourite old loom in the Weaver's Cottage. The workload from raw wool to finished product took her some three months. It was only later I found out that she had woven it on Willie Meikle's loom, the very one I had read about in Morton's work many years before. Everything is connected in some way. From Wallace to the present day, and all the Scots in between, there is a connecting thread running through the history of the plaid that is Scotland.

I have sat and watched Christine weave, the shuttle flying from side to side across the loom. I find it soothing, that clack-clack-clack. It has been heard in Scotland over many centuries, although very seldom now. I remember finding a headstone in the graveyard that clusters around the little church at Arbuthnott near Inverbervie, where Lewis Grassic Gibbon, that great Scottish writer, is buried. There was a shape carved upon the stone, an item I recognised to be the same as the thing that flew across Christine's loom. The inscription read: 'The days of my life fly like the weaver's shuttle.' And they do. I don't know where the time goes. So much I want to see and do. I, like many others, have had health scares, and I hope that I get a chance to put at least some of the plans I have into place.

You have probably heard the expression 'the full nine yards', and it comes from the size of the old plaids. Christine indeed wove mine nine yards long, but you wear it 'double width', so I needed someone to cut it in half and sew the two halves together to make the correct width for the finished plaid. This was standard practice, as the old looms only wove to 3ft or 3ft 6ins wide. Christine was scared, but again I was lucky enough to know the right person. My mate Jim Singer runs the Aberdeen Wallace Day, and his wife Elma makes up plaids and sews kilts for a lot of the boys (by 'the boys', I mean all the patriots I know) and she cut and sewed up my plaid. She did a brilliant job, and the join is invisible. I will be wearing this plaid when I leave Robroyston on 3 August 2005, and I will be wearing it in London on the twenty-third. It will probably be worn to death for many years to come, my 'Wallace' plaid. Then it will be put in a glass case to hang on the wall or similar, just so my grandchildren can say, 'That's what that boring old bugger wore for Wallace's 700th anniversary commemoration.' But it does mean a lot to me.

Being Scottish, I am either maudlin and near to greetin' about something, or wanting to kick someone's teeth in. When I was given the plaid I was so touched that when I tried to speak the words caught in my throat. I was really upset till I got angry at someone and cheered up again!

So what was I going to do with this coffin I was bringing back from London, filled with its many messages? Pure coincidence had Margo Steele phone me from Lanark to ask for some input on a Wallace-related project. I told her a little about my plans with the coffin for the 700th anniversary, and this started the ball rolling. Others from Lanark Council came on board – Frank Gunning,

George Topp, etc. – and they expressed a desire to have the coffin taken to St Kentigern's Church in the town. Again, I was really pleased. Legend tells us that it was in this very church that Wallace first set eyes on his sweetheart Marion, and that they were married in this same building. It is ruined now, but there are plans afoot to reconstruct one of the outbuildings to form a last resting place for the coffin. Somewhere for people to visit and reflect. Somewhere for those who care about Scotland to consider their nation's future.

And I would never be able to envisage a project such as this without Elspeth King being involved! Elspeth is the curator at the Stirling Smith Art Gallery and Museum. She has a genius in putting together exhibitions that the ordinary 'real' people of Scotland want to see. She had intended to try and beg, borrow or get a loan of as many Wallace artefacts as possible for an exhibition on the man to coincide with August 2005. When I spoke to her about the coffin she immediately asked to have it in the Stirling Smith. This worked on several levels, but importantly it gave what I was trying to do an artistic quality too. Many of the people who were not able to make London, for whatever reasons, would at least be able to go to Stirling to see the coffin, and they would also be able to leave notes for the church in London, just as I had envisaged. So everyone has a chance to make their connection with Wallace.

Andy Hillhouse comes from Cockenzie in East Lothian. His paintings of the time of the Wars of Independence have to be seen to be believed. Andy did a work called the *Spirit of Wallace*, and as soon as I saw it I knew it fitted the Wallace commemorations perfectly. Hence it is on the cover of this book. This picture was also on the ticket that allowed admission to the church service at St Bart's. Lynn Boland Richardson, a Canadian of Scots blood, who I met through the Highland Games circuit in Canada, was good enough to get the tickets designed and printed up.

There are a hundred others who helped in some small way who I have not mentioned here, especially in the Society of William Wallace, which, as you can imagine, backed this project to the hilt. I thank each and every one of you.

I know this all sounds as if it went swimmingly and everyone pulled together. But we must always remember that Wallace himself was betrayed by a Scot. And it seems that not a lot has changed in 700 years. As soon as I announced the plans for the commemoration, hate mail started to appear. Some to the Society of William Wallace and, even more worryingly, some to St Bart's in London. You can imagine the gist, one saying that they would make sure I never reached the border. Yeah, right. I have trained this hard to be a 6ft 5ins, 17 stone pushover. But the most twisted thing of all was the fact they used false names and addresses. I wouldn't have expected them to use their real names and addresses, right enough! And the fact that they were sometimes signed 'The Real Tartan Army.' What a slur on the greatest group of football supporters on the planet! Unionism at its best. But this was a small minority, and many more people came on-side. I was a little scared at first that folk might think all this to be a bizarre idea, but it seems the Lion of Scotland is still in the hearts and minds of her sons and daughters. And it seems that many of them care just as I do.

CHAPTER TEN

The Walk Begins

I STOOD AND LOOKED at the Robroyston Monument, which was raised in 1900 to mark the site of Wallace's capture. I sighed a little, trying to cast my mind back to this day exactly 700 years before – 3 August 1305. A wee crowd had gathered to see me off, and of course to pay their respects to the man himself on the anniversary of his capture. There were television cameras, and I did a few interviews, said a few words in front of the monument, then it was time to go. I had on the plaid that Chris had made for me and so it was just a case of best foot forward, and off I went. Lots of people asked if I was going to wear the plaid on the whole journey, but the simple answer was 'no'. The plaid is a very warm garment, and can be worn in several different ways to suit conditions, but I had to try and complete this walk within the time scale and modern clothing was my choice. In fact several Scotland football tops and shorts were my chosen garb for most of the journey, along with a hat of some sort.

I had a co-pilot in the shape of my fellow patriot Dennis McGhee. Dennis was driving the van that was to accompany me on my journey. And an old friend, Billy Sutherland, organised the van itself. Billy runs a hire company in Dumfries, and sorted out the loan of a long wheelbase Renault van for me, again free of charge. This was a huge help. Dennis and I decided to sleep in the van as we did not want to stay in hotels and the like because firstly, we did not have the money, secondly, that would have seemed soft somehow when you consider what Wallace went through, and thirdly, it meant I was not held to any routine and could walk as far as I could manage every day. The van was no slouch either, with a diesel turbo engine that could eat many cars on the road for breakfast with its turn of speed. Thanks, Billy – you made bits of the journey fun too!

Dennis is a coachbuilder by trade and he tricked up the back of the van, boxing the coffin in under my bed and creating a foldaway bunk for himself, as well as rigging up a cooker of sorts. All very comfy.

I should perhaps mention at this point that I had received the accolade of knighthood from Prince Michael of Albany. When I was approached and asked if I was amenable to this ennoblement I was caught by surprise. I was told that the Prince had decided that I should enter England with the same title that Wallace had held. In fact, I was knighted on the same spot as Wallace, in the Kirk of the Forest in Selkirk.

I did think about this long and hard beforehand. I looked at what knighthood actually meant in its original form, where it was given for defence of one's country. It has been corrupted over the years of course, and is equated with money and position today. But I looked at it as a sign of patriotism, knowing that I would do all I could for Scotland and its freedom under any circumstances. So the Prince knighted me just a few days before I set off. It gave me something to think about, as I walked that long road to the border. But before the border could be approached I had other duties to perform.

So I walked the mile or so up to the Asda supermarket near the A80 Glasgow to Stirling road, and then Dennis picked me up and we drove down to Glasgow's George Square where I was to get a civic send-off from the City Chambers. This seemed to consist merely of me getting my photo taken many hundreds of times by a small crowd of photographers. Quite bizarre. I was asked to do all sorts of things, most of which involved contrived posing like jumping in the air or sitting with my legs in the sky. I had to gently remind the snappers that this was all being done in commemoration of William Wallace and what he went through, and I was not really up for this sort of thing. I knew some of it had to be done though, because first and foremost I was trying to let the people of Scotland know that it was the anniversary of the murder of their national hero, but it can be like balancing on a knife-edge, keeping it on the right side of good taste.

Eventually I managed to walk away from 'just one more shot', and Dennis drove me back up to the Asda, where I continued to walk.

I had no preconceived route in mind, just a rough idea inside my head, but it worked out okay in the end. I crossed the M8 on a footbridge and headed for Glasgow Celtic's football stadium and nearby London Road, which, as its name suggests, is the old main route heading south. Once on London Road, I just walked the old road to England. Right out of Glasgow and through Uddingston and Bothwell, crossing Bothwell Bridge with its monument to the battle there in the 1600s, and then on into Hamilton and Larkhall, walking past Dennis's front door! As I passed Canderside Toll and onto a much quieter stretch of the old A74, which now carries the designation B7076, I reached a point where I could see Glasgow some 20 miles behind me, nestling in Clydesdale, then I was over the lip of the hill and had left it behind, and the road stretched away to the south.

We do not know the route that Wallace was taken south, but old A roads are generally on ancient routes, some used for thousands of years. I don't think Wallace was taken to the border on a well-trodden path, although after Carlisle the A6 is the most likely route.

So it was just a case of trudging on, putting one foot in front of the other, head down, hitting the wall, pushing on through the pain, and walking some more. Sometimes I would catch a couple of hours sleep during the day, especially if it was particularly hot, and walk into the night.

Through Blackwood, Lesmahagow, crossing the Douglas Water and glancing upstream towards Douglas village and St Bride's Kirk, where I knew the mighty Good Sir James Douglas, companion of the Bruce, was buried. Up onto the moors and on to Abington and Crawford. I glanced across the now very picturesque Clyde to the trees, beyond which I knew Crawford Castle stood. Blind Harry tells us that Wallace burnt this place and slew its English garrison. Its ruins stand on a knoll, reached by a road and bridge from the village.

A little further and I crossed the Clyde again, by the old bridge a mile or so beyond Crawford, just past the Elvanfoot turn off. I always tend to pause and peer down into the water when I cross rivers and streams. The Clyde is clear, shallow and stony here, and I watched it eddy across its rough bed, when I noticed there was a chain poking through the grass on the southern, downstream side of the bridge. I couldn't see a path down, but I scrambled down the steep embankment, much to the concern of my tired legs.

I discovered that the heavy chain circled an old forgotten grave-yard. I pulled and kicked at the heavy growth of summer grass, and discovered a little scatter of graves, and a bigger stone telling some of the story. These were men killed in the construction of the rail-way between Carlisle and Glasgow in the 1800s, and this little bit of ground right beside the river had been consecrated to serve as their last resting place. Perhaps they were Irish navvies, come to seek a wage, and had been killed in a blast gone wrong. Perhaps their families waited in vain for news or for their return. There were no marks through the scrub surrounding this spot to show that anyone had been near the place for years, so I promised myself I'd come back in the winter, or with a petrol strimmer to cut back the grass, and have a good look at a later date.

A mile or two further and I was level with the source of the Clyde. I remember reading books by the great Glasgow author Jack House when I was relatively young. Jack said somewhere that he had walked from the source of the Clyde to Glasgow two or three times, and I thought that this was an extraordinary thing. I could not really envisage a walk of that distance or the effort involved. It just seemed amazing to me. Now, the Clyde meanders in its route, away over to Lanark for instance, and I had taken a direct route south, but I had walked from Robroyston to the source of the Clyde in only thirteen or fourteen walking hours in total! I could-n't really get to grips with this.

It was at this point that I really began to think about marching in terms of a medieval army. I realised the distances a determined army could cover in pursuit of their goal, and it occurred to me that 90% of an army's waking hours would have been spent on the hoof.

I was using a route that many armies would have used in the past too, as I followed the A74 from Clydesdale over into Annandale, reaching the village of Beattock. I had come through the Southern Uplands of Scotland at this point, and was onto flatter, straighter roads.

Dennis drove a few miles at a time, and simply waited for me to catch him up. If I needed anything – food or water, or even a short sleep – I could get it, then he would move on. He was brilliant, as he treated the whole situation as a job of work and not just a jaunt. Again and again he would say, 'Dave, you just walk. I'll do my best to take care of everything else.' And he did. He always had hot water ready for tea or coffee, went to the nearest launderette if there was one, and cooked dinners. I had been expecting to have to try and find take-aways to eat, but Dennis often had steak with all the trimmings or a stew ready for me. I actually ate better on the walk than I usually did at home. When any of the boys called my mobile I would tell them how well I was being looked after. With the wicked sense of humour that permeates my patriot friends, they bought him a French maid's outfit after the walk. He took the banter with good grace!

As I passed through Johnstonebridge I noticed the plaque from the original bridge over the River Annan, built by Thomas Telford, the great engineer, was now bolted to the modern replacement. At the pace I was setting, close on 30 miles a day, I knew that I would cross the border on my fourth day.

Each night, when I wanted to sleep, Dennis picked me up and we found a quiet spot and I immediately fell into a deep sleep. I would generally sleep about nine or ten hours on the walk, and when I was not eating, all of my time, and I mean all, was spent walking. Every morning after I rose, I would ensure I returned to the exact spot where I had finished the day before, to resume the punishment.

Sometimes my thoughts would turn to Wallace, and I would go over his final journey in my mind – especially as I neared England.

Between Lockerbie – site of the terrible terrorist outrage where a jumbo jet was brought down into the town – and Ecclefechan, I caught sight of the hills of England's Lake District in the distance, just as Wallace must have done.

Then I reached Gretna and the border. As I said earlier, the class at Armadale Primary School in West Lothian had a contest to design a t-shirt for the walk. I promised the boy who won, Fraser Keast, that I would wear his winning design as I crossed the border, so I changed into it as I stepped into England.

At the south end of Gretna, famous for its runaway marriages in times past, you can see across the Solway Firth to the spot where Edward Longshanks breathed his last. I contemplated this as I stepped into England, and thought of poor Wallace leaving Scotland forever, 700 years before. There must have been a moment when he knew he was in England. And knew that he would never see Scotland again.

Now the road, all the way from Glasgow to the border, has been upgraded to motorway, so I was able to walk the quiet old roads. But the motorway network in England stops at Carlisle. The English authorities have never bothered upgrading the road north of their northernmost city, Carlisle, to the Scottish border. And why should they? The Scottish politicians are too gutless to take a stand, and the people, dare I say it, too blinkered to vote for anything other than Unionist parties, so I suppose they deserve to be treated as an ethnic minority. Anyone else would cry 'racism!' of course, but the Scots seem to like to lie down to be kicked, or some of them do at least. So rather than take a long detour I decided to walk the ten miles or so to Carlisle on the grass verge with the traffic thundering by. Wasn't too bad until the heavens opened. Grass soaked through my shoes and socks in seconds. I tried walking at the edge of the road, but it was suicidal. Ended up wet and filthy. I cut through some trees at one point, where I put up some deer. One got its antlered head caught in a wire fence and it thrashed and crashed trying to break free, and about 50 metres of fence was shaking with its efforts. I could never have walked away and left it, so I approached to try and get it out. It didn't appreciate this

Scotsman's close proximity of course, and redoubled its efforts. I had one foot against its flank to try and stop it struggling, one hand on the wire, and one gripping an antler to manoeuvre it out – and to stop it goring me. I couldn't do it, but did not want to leave it. Then a wee light went on in my head and I walked away, crossed the fence a good bit down, then approached the deer head on. It pulled away from me this time of course, and this helped me turn its antlers by brute force and free it. It took off in bounds like a springbok, crashing away through the undergrowth in 10-foot high leaps.

Good deed done, I struggled on to Carlisle. I walked past the castle and again my mind turned to Wallace. It was here he was handed over to Segrave for the journey south to London. The same keep, dour and stark, that Wallace saw stands here still, and I'm sure he could not have missed the old cathedral, which stands only a stone's throw from the castle. He had been to the castle before, during his invasion of northern England after the victory at Stirling Bridge in 1297.

I could follow quieter roads south from here, and I walked under the M6 and reached the lovely little village of Wreay. This was the one real bonus of the walk, discovering unspoilt little villages, usually clustered around their old churches. But I noticed that from Carlisle south, there was a wealth on show that had no equivalent at home. So many manors and granges, and property prices that were astronomical compared to poorer Scotland. Not everywhere of course, city sprawl being more or less the same in both nations, but the signs of a different level of wealth were in evidence. Classic cars, for example. There seemed to be many in garages and driveways, to be taken out and enjoyed on a Sunday. I have never seen the equivalent here. This is not the fault of the English, I hasten to add! Good luck to them. But so many Scots put up with having the economy of another nation forced upon their own, and inequality of wealth is a result of that.

I crossed back under the M6 just after Southwaite Services, and walked the country road that closely aligns the M6 to its west. I walked the last few miles into Penrith on the A6, but not before I had stood in the infant River Petteril to try and cool down my lightly sunburned legs.

I was now in the footsteps of Bonnie Prince Charlie's army of 1745, and going from town to town as he did. I followed the A6 south from Penrith, passing some ancient sites, one of which the locals once believed to be King Arthur's Round Table, which is signposted just after you have crossed Eamont Bridge.

Then you climb to the long straggle of houses that comprise the village of Clifton. You have the ancient church on your left – which features the stone to the dead of 'Bland's Regiment', the redcoats killed in the battle here, fought between Charles and Cumberland – and the old castellated tower of Clifton Hall is on your right.

At the southern end of the village there are a few memorials to the battle in the inshot on your right. A path runs off to your left, and if you follow it you'll find the brave Highlanders who were slain in this encounter, buried under an ancient oak tree, with a stone marking the spot. I've been here a few times now, with patriot friends, and the pipes have been played, and muskets fired in salute.

So many cars and lorries from the north fly by on the nearby M6, oblivious to their fellow countrymen lying for eternity in foreign soil.

I knew the A6 ahead of here would be difficult to walk. It has steep grassy sides and no pavements. I had noticed this on previous journeys south. Obviously, once I had the idea of the walk in my mind, I started to notice the difficulties I would face any time I ventured over the border. So I cut onto little side roads and walked through two delightful villages, Great Strickland and Little Strickland.

The roads climbed up towards Shap Summit, then eventually petered out at the side of an enormous quarry. I skirted the eastern side of it, peering down over its sheer sides occasionally, down into its depths, where many hundreds of gulls were gathered, and a pair of buzzards circled overhead.

An old path continued over the hills, which in part followed the course of an old Roman road. When I thought about the age of this thoroughfare, I wondered if I were walking the route exactly as Wallace had walked it. It was not bad going, with absolutely tremendous views to both east and west, 1,500 feet up as I was, but I was glad the ground was dry, as I think it would have been a sucking, filthy trek after rain.

This was the only bit of the journey that I did not cover on metalled road surfaces of some sort.

I followed the path over to Tebay Services on the M6, and crossed the motorway by the bridge there. I followed the old road on and over towards Kendal, initially sharing the valley of the River Lune with the M6 and the West Coast Railway Line.

The road climbed, and I cut onto small country roads to take me towards Oxenholme, just east of Kendal itself. Whether through tiredness or the lie of the land, I really struggled for the last few miles. The rolling dales may be interesting to look at, but the punishment I took with the constantly changing gradients knocked the stuffing out of me. It was a case of eyes shut and just placing one foot in front of the other till I could go no further that day. Luckily I have a sister who stays in Kendal, and Diane let me filthy her bath and fed me well, and I slept in a bed instead of the van for the first time since I set off.

Refreshed the next morning, it was back to covering the miles again. Don't get me wrong though. Every day was a push through the stiffness and pain till I found my stride again. Sometimes it took an hour before my body adjusted and I took on a steady pace.

I had noticed that the northernmost part of the Lancaster Canal began just a few miles south of Kendal, and as the idea of walking a canal towpath really appealed to me, I headed down country lanes till I reached it.

I had often considered the extensive canal network in England as I tried to put together some idea of the walk together in my head. The lap of water, barges pottering past, the wildlife, the fact that there would be very little in the way of gradients; it sounded perfect, and I looked forward to covering the miles away from traffic and in relative comfort.

So I reached the canal, and was surprised that there was so little wear and tear. The towpath was grassy, and I didn't see anyone else on the first few miles of walking. Carrying a mobile phone made contact between Dennis and me no problem, and if I needed anything from him I could catch up with him at the many road bridges the canal passed under.

After several miles I discovered why the canal was so quiet and why I had not seen a single craft on my journey. It came to the M6 and just stopped! When the M6 was constructed it was put right through the canal, which could be seen continuing on the other side. On my Ordnance Survey map, it looked as though the canal travels under the motorway, but that was not the case. No wonder I had seen no traffic.

I had to scramble over the fence onto the hard shoulder of the motorway to get into a field where I could scramble through to the nearest A road. I hoped that the police would not come along and arrest me for jaywalking. Folk have actually said to me since, 'Why didn't you just run across the motorway to the other side?' On the M6!? I may be bonkers sometimes, but I don't have a death wish.

Anyway, I ploughtered through fields till I reached the A6 running south, and decided that I would take my chances with the traffic rather than trust the vagaries of the canal network.

Burton was a nice village, and I bought some goodies from a shop and sat on the handily placed bench at the south end of the village for a munch before pushing on.

Dennis would leapfrog me constantly to make sure I was okay. The van became my lifeline, and as the days went on I formed a real attachment to it. It was my wee sanctuary, and catching sight of its nose sticking out of a side lane gladdened my heart.

Strange that just 100 years ago, if you could not afford a horse – or a motor car – you had to walk if you wanted to get anywhere, yet in 2005 I would cover mile after mile with traffic thundering by and would never see another soul.

At night as I collapsed into my bunk, knowing the coffin was tucked up underneath me, draped in tartan rugs and a Saltire or two, Dennis would usually regale me with a story of his extremely mis-spent past. Brilliant stories, most of them, outrageous in their content, and I'll probably get mileage out of retelling them for the rest of my days.

And speaking of days, they had started to blur. Each morning it took longer to get into a stride, and texts and calls would ask 'What have you seen?' but it was just turning into a daily grind, and I would not divert from my path to look at something 50 feet away, as that 50 feet would be better spent walking forward. So the answer to the question 'What have you seen?' was 'Not very much!'

I could see the sea away to my right, which made London seem very far away, as it is near the opposite coast in the south east, but I followed the A6 on to Lancaster with its mighty castle, and cast my mind back to the times of King Robert Bruce, as his armies would often raid this far south.

I remember there was a wee row of cherry trees between Lancaster and Garstang, and I picked a handful of cherries and ate them as I walked. They were beautiful. Succulent and juicy. In fact I picked quite a lot of berries en route and munched away at them, as probably many a medieval soldier did on long marches. This made me think of Bonnie Prince Charlie's army, and the fact that they marched through the winter of 1745/6, so there was nothing for them to take off the bushes in passing.

It made me wonder if Wallace, hungry and parched, looked with longing at the brambles in passing, as of course he would have been en route at the same time of year as me.

What I did notice is that by the time I reached south east England, the brambles were well past their best. It had been warm and they had ripened early there.

On to Preston, reached by the Jacobites in 1715. I crossed the River Ribble and headed on to cross the M6, still keeping to the route of the A6. I passed through Chorley, and even though I am writing this only a couple of weeks after the fact, I cannot remember a thing about the place. It was getting to the stage where I was walking into unknown territory and I can remember that my mind was starting to go to a strange place. Walking was everything. My whole existence. It was as if I was drugged. I have since spoken to long distance runners and they tell me the same thing. They run through the pain barrier, and it is only an autopilot response that keeps them going, their mind so focused on the task ahead that their senses change completely.

I remember walking well into the night and finally collapsing into bed near a village called Westhoughton.

The next day I carried on through Salford and into Manchester. There was a sudden downpour of ridiculously heavy rain, but I was only yards from a railway bridge at the time, and I hid there till it passed, marvelling at the absolute wall of water coming down at either side of my shelter.

I lost Dennis in Manchester, as I was walking straight through and he was following the ring road. We agreed to meet at the start of the A6 as it comes out of Manchester and heads for Stockport. I passed signs proclaiming that I was near the Arndale Centre, the main shopping mall, which I knew from a previous visit when writing the *On the Trail of Bonnie Prince Charlie* book.

A little further and I did not recognise any of the destinations on the road signs, and could not spot the A6 or Stockport mentioned anywhere. I was lost, so asked passers-by how to get to the Stockport road.

I had passed it by miles, and had to double back, making frantic calls on the mobile to Dennis to try and get my bearings. The realisation that I had walked too far in one direction made every step an effort and my legs were made of lead. It had got to the stage where mistakes were costing me dear mentally, as an absolute pervading exhaustion was starting to creep in, but luckily I never made another as bad as the one in Manchester.

I constantly walked by wee curry houses and the like. Nothing flash, just a counter and a few metal tables like a café, but they smelled so good and were dirt-cheap. I promised myself that Dennis and I would eat in one that night, and that thought pushed me on till I reached Stockport.

Dennis went visiting at one point during the day. He had a bad drink problem at one time and had ended up in a dry-out centre in the Stockport area. He has never touched a drop since, a good point in a driver on a trip like this. He knocked on the door, and told them what we were up to, and asked if it would be all right if he came back with me later in the day to get cleaned up and the like?

Although none of the staff were there from his sojourn years before, he was able to name names of people they knew and they let us in.

There was a huge Victorian bathtub and it was bliss to lie in it in my exhausted state, and get shaved and feel clean for the first time in days.

Dennis told me that he had made enquiries about the other folk that had been in residence at the same time as him, and it turned out nearly every one of them was dead. This obviously affected him and I remember just before I slept that night telling him something along the lines of, 'You survived for a reason, Dennis. What we are doing here is so important, a message for all Scotland, that you were meant to pull through from your old life to help achieve what we are aiming at here – to bring back the spirit of Wallace and some self respect for Scotland.' I hope he appreciated that. So much of the detail for the walk and the commemoration fell into place like it was meant to be, that I believed that Dennis, like me, had a job to do, and we survived this long to get this tribute to Wallace done.

We finally got our curries that night, by the way.

I crossed the infant River Mersey at Stockport and knew that I was past halfway.

I noticed that, while most signs in Scotland give you the name of the town ahead and then the mileage, those in England, on these A designation roads at least, only tell you the towns ahead, but never the mileage. I found this a bit of a pain, as I like to be kept informed!

As soon as I left Stockport behind, the road really began to climb, and I spent a whole day just walking uphill. I spotted an old black and white striped direction pole, quite rusted, but it had a bit of information on it that I found amazing. One arm said 'London, 182 miles, A6.' I had covered something like 250 miles in well under nine days. I could not believe I had achieved this, even if I had gone through the heels of a pair of my shoes.

London lies in the south east. I did not fancy the trek down to Birmingham for some reason, and the A6 seemed to consistently have a pavement or at least a line I could walk within, so I had decided to stick with it. But this now meant a long hard slog up and over the Pennines, that range of hills knows as the 'Backbone of England', to reach England's soft underbelly and hopefully a much flatter route down to London.

The scenery improved admittedly, and I had hills to look at. Being Scottish, I always feel somehow more contented when I have hills around me. Flat fields and hedgerows just don't do it for me I'm afraid.

But it was a constant uphill slog, with one 'improved' stretch meaning I had no pavement and had to take my chances on the white lined verge of a dual carriageway.

I climbed towards Chapel en le Frith in the Peak District, and as I walked a piece where the road was constricted in a little pass, I noticed a sign which, unusually, had a mileage on it, stating 'Buxton 5'. As I knew that less than an hour and a half would have me in a sizeable community, I pressed on, but 20 minutes or so later I came across another sign that stated 'Buxton 5'. I could do without these types of mind games!

Those last few miles into Buxton were a real low point. It was across high moorland with traffic thundering by. I was suddenly incredibly cold, but sweating profusely.

I had phoned Dennis, and he said he would come and get me if I wished, but I knew he was cooking in the back of the van and told him I would carry on till I reached him at Buxton. I couldn't stop shaking, and the wind cut me to the bone. I found a golf club cover lying in the verge, a woolly affair, and I put my hands into it just to keep them warm. I staggered the last few miles and when I spotted the van it was like I had discovered an oasis in the desert. Dennis had cooked a stew, and I barely finished it before I went out like a light. I had hit the wall with a vengeance.

Going uphill for so many, many miles had finished me, for that day at least. A good sleep though, and I was ready to continue.

I intended to follow the A6 towards Matlock, but for some reason we decided to do a wee recce forwards a few miles to look at the road. Just as well. It twisted and turned down a rocky pass with steep banks on either side. Articulated lorries thundered by, missing each other by inches. Dennis said, 'You can't walk this Dave, it's suicidal.' He was right. There was just no room, so I looked at the map and decided to take the A515 to Ashbourne. It too had no pavement, but at least it was wide and straight, and I could walk facing the oncoming traffic.

There seemed to be many prehistoric remains in this hilly area, and at one point when I stopped for a snack and a drink, we decided to drive back a mile or so to have a look at Arbor Low Henge, known as the 'Stonehenge of the North.'

Very impressive. There were many huge stones within the circular earthworks, but they had all fallen. Great views out over the surrounding countryside too. In fact, there were many stretches on this raised bit of the route where I had a panorama outwards of some 20 miles.

After the visit to the henge, when Dennis dropped me at my original stopping point to start walking again, a crash happened right in front of us, a car turning out of a pub car park pulling out in front of an oncoming vehicle. Bit of a mess, but at least everyone walked away from it, and any crash you walk away from is a 'good' crash! Third crash I had seen on the walk. A bus hit a van at a junction, and I watched two girls in a little Vauxhall Corsa pull out of a lane just feet in front of an articulated lorry, which whacked the car sideways several feet down the road. Both of these happened in Manchester, within five minutes walking of one another. See the things you see when you are out and about?

Nobody hurt, I'm glad to say.

On the last ten miles down to Ashbourne there were many steep downhill gradients, as I started to leave England's Peak District behind and move towards its flat underbelly.

On one of these downhills I watched a white Volvo pass slowly, turn and come crawling back towards me. As it passed, one of the passengers threw a banger at me. I reported this to some friends and the details were published on a couple of websites. Because I had said 'banger', people remarked that it was bizarre folk were throwing sausages at me, but I actually meant a firework!

Another common occurrence was people driving towards me and, when they were just a foot or two away, leaning sharply on their horn to try to give me a fright. But it became so commonplace I never even flinched.

On nice days, while he was waiting for me, Dennis would park in lay-bys and get out a collapsible sun lounger he had in the van, to pass the time and catch a few rays. Folk would drive by and lean their horns constantly, obviously a little teed-off that they were working, and, 'Look at that so and so lying relaxing.'

The worst was when I had to walk at the roadside facing on-coming traffic, and I would see vehicles, generally transitsized vans coming towards me, and I could see them veering in as their drivers tried to clip me with their large black wing mirrors.

Now, one or two I actually felt the wind of as they missed me by a millimetre, and several times I had to throw myself onto the grass. And if I were honest, if I had a bazooka on my person I would have blown their vans off the face of the Earth. It was obviously just a bit of sport to Neanderthal drivers, but if they had actually caught me at 60 miles per hour they would have torn my face off, and it would have been a murder charge. But I'm sure they didn't think it through that deeply.

Downhill to Ashbourne, then. It is a lovely wee place. I had been there twice before, following Bonnie Prince Charlie's route to Derby. The elegant church has some magnificent tombs, one or two of which contain gentlemen who fought against the Scots; one at Flodden in 1513, I recall.

Ashbourne has many old buildings, and just across from the church is a school founded by Elizabeth I which has centuries of carved graffiti on its walls.

But other than the place itself, what really caught my attention was the number of St George's Cross flags of England on display. Every single building in the centre of town had one flying from its frontage. When you looked down the streets they were a riot of red and white. I couldn't think of an equivalent in Scotland.

There has been much debate in the press recently about whether the English have an identity or not, and whether they really know what and who they are. The answer is a very positive 'yes!' The English to me know exactly who they are. Everywhere I went I saw St George's Crosses. In fact, hundreds of them on the walk. I saw only a few Union Jacks. I could probably have counted them on one hand. About the only places the Union Flag still flies is in Northern Ireland and at Glasgow's Ibrox Park. Why? I don't really know.

The English have an ever strengthening identity, and that identity is not British. About one in five people I passed had on a top that identified their Englishness in some way. Football tops, polo shirts with the three leopards of England on them, or a t-shirt that simply said 'England.'

When I passed parks or playgrounds I began to notice that there was always a plethora of red and white clothing on show. Kids wearing red and white. The colour of England. They are so aware of who they are that I realised that it is Scotland that is being left behind. There are those here that hang on to their Union Jacks or Irish tricolours, or have that horrific Scottish cringe whenever national identity is mentioned, when our towns should be bedecked with the white cross of St Andrew on blue, shouting and proclaiming what we are.

I left Ashbourne behind and headed on towards Derby. Derby had been stuck in my mind for a long time, I think simply because Charlie had reached there in 1745, and it formed that sort of barrier of being the 'furthest south the Scots had ever reached' in my head, so if I could pass there I would feel that I was really pushing on, plus I knew London was only some 130 miles south of Derby.

Blistering was proving to be a problem. It was not choice of footwear or socks that was causing it though. It seemed to be my bodyweight pressing down more than anything else. As I already said, I am not really the right size and shape for long distance stuff, although I passed a gym and asked if I could weigh myself about halfway through the walk, and I had dropped from 110 kilos to about 99. I had not really eaten that day though, which I'm sure would make a small difference. I sometimes found that I had three or four mouthfuls and just didn't fancy eating any more, but I went through lots of water.

I kept lancing the blisters and taping them up after I had cleaned them, and hoped I could hold out to the end.

I pushed on through Derby, diverting just a few yards to see the equestrian statue of Bonnie Prince Charlie; the only statue of Charlie that I know of, and surprisingly enough it stands in England!

I walked by the pub where Charlie took up residence, and pressed on hard for the Swarkestone Bridge over the River Trent, another six miles south.

I was tired but walked through the southern suburbs of Derby, crossed the A50 and went on to Swarkstone. Charlie's advance guard took this vital bridge, its ancient causeway leading south across the flood plain of the Trent.

The advance guard was apparently nonplussed when the order came to retreat, as the road was open to London. Charlie's officers had believed the propaganda of advancing government forces and they insisted, against Charlie's wishes, on a retreat. I wanted to cross the bridge and walk on.

You can stand there and watch the deep dark Trent flow sluggishly under the old stonework, just as the tartan clad Highlanders did 260 years before. There is a cairn commemorating this fact in the garden of the pub, which runs down to the riverside.

I walked over the bridge with Dennis, so we had done what we came to do, but then we jumped back into the van and retraced the route a mile or two, so I could then cut over to the A6 again to follow it south. I had a network of cycle paths to walk to reach Kegworth, which I remember had a beautiful old church, and I pushed on towards Loughborough. Planes flew over, heading for East Midlands Airport. Strange that. Only a few days before I had been in Manchester and Stockport, which the English regard as the north west, and some twenty-five hours' walking later I was in the East Midlands and making good progress south.

I was walking through pain barriers constantly now. I got second winds though; or if I were really suffering I would just lie down in my bunk, the coffin tucked underneath, and sleep till I woke, and begin walking again. There was always a little more spirit to pull on, and I remember saying over and over to Dennis that I just wanted to see a sign that told me London was less than 100 miles away. I knew Leicester was 97, but I wanted to see a sign that said so!

By now, my head had gone to a really strange place. I had become an automaton. I walked, I slept, and the only other thing I did was eat, and that was only a few minutes of my day. I saw nothing much but the road about ten feet in front of me. My mind was miles away. So much so that as I walked towards Leicester, deviating slightly through Mountsorrel, a cyclist, unheard, came up behind me. Traffic was rumbling by. I just put one foot in front of the other hour after hour, and I was so far gone I never heard him approach. He said right behind me, 'Excuse me!' and I almost died of fright. It was like a voice from the heavens and I was so far away that it took me a few seconds to realise where it had come from.

I envied the odd cyclist who passed me. They seemed to cover the ground so fast and disappear into the distance. On the odd occasion I was in the van with Dennis, even 20 miles per hour seemed ridiculously fast, so used was I to my walking pace.

I remember as I walked through Leicester I saw signs pointing to my left that proclaimed 'Abbey Ruins'. I really wanted to see things like that, but I never deviated. I just plodded on. One day soon I will go over the route again on a motorcycle and I will look at all the things I would normally have looked at.

If it were not too far, I would get Dennis to drive me to a nearby swimming bath after I had finished walking, as they were usually open quite late in the evening. Each day I walked, at the very least, 25 plus miles. I had a few well over 30 mile days, but somewhere near 30, in the high 20s, was my usual.

I had gone through the heels of two pairs of my Nike Shox by this time, too.

In the baths I would usually just stand in the water, and that sensation of weightlessness was so brilliant after the walking that it seemed like heaven. The chemicals dried my blisters out, too. I stood in the shower with my filthy Scotland football top and shorts on to clean out the grime, and got many a strange look, but I was beyond caring. When I left the building, clean and shaven, it made me feel like carrying on a little further.

We visited the swimming pool in Market Harborough, but it was earlier than usual and the place was packed, which was no fun. The town itself looked nice and worth revisiting for a wander at some point. The place had a wealthy feel to it, and to me, as a Scot, a very *south east* ambience, and I felt that London was drawing near.

I was well under the 100 mile mark now and eager to stop this endless torture, and I remember pushing myself on to reach Kettering, the last few miles spent walking the edge of an incredibly busy stretch of dual carriageway. It was on this stretch that I had my one and only offer of a lift. I thanked the guy profusely, but declined, much to his surprise I think, and wandered on.

The signs welcoming me to shire after shire were passing with the days. I saw I was now in Northamptonshire and eventually reached Kettering.

We parked in a supermarket car park for the night, which was a sensible thing to do, as we could go in for a reasonably priced breakfast in the morning, and get washed too.

On the way out in the morning rush hour I passed an amazing looking park with lots of attractions; Wickstead Park. This name gave me a flashback. I recalled that the thick iron-made slides in parks, chutes as we Scots call them, had steps with writing on them. They were sort of wrought iron, obviously made in a mould of sorts, and I remembered they said 'Wickstead and Kettering' on them. Another childhood mystery solved!

It was only much later, when I looked at maps of the route, that I discovered that Geddington, with its original Eleanor Cross, was near to Kettering, and I would have liked to have visited it. (The Eleanor Crosses, as I said before, were raised to mark where the body of Longshanks' wife rested on its way to London from Lincolnshire.)

Bedford was the next port of call. On the never-ending stretch of dual carriageway there were actually mileage signs, and I plodded by each one. 'Bedford 10', 'Bedford 9', etc. till I reached the town itself. I was incredibly tired by this time, the pace taking its toll, but I never wanted to stop. I always felt I could walk another three or four miles before sleep, probably because I knew London was nearer with every step, and I could almost sense its nearness now. I can remember Dennis forcing me to stop somewhere around Bedford, telling me that I had been reeling for the last few miles, and kept dropping to one knee before staggering on.

I did notice one thing from here on, too, even through the now constant pain. There were stickers bearing St George's crosses on poles at the roadside, advocating an English parliament. Good luck to them. The more the English wake up to their sense of nationhood, the more likely Scotland is to go its own way.

Next was Luton, Bedfordshire, and the accents sounded decidedly Londonish now. I was really, really exhausted. I could remember very little of what I had walked by during the day. Luton itself was a blur.

My feet were a shambles now. The blisters were becoming very bloody. I was scared to stop as I took so long fighting against the pain to get started again. I had to take time to patch and pad my feet each morning before I could carry on.

But every time I thought about why I was doing this, in memory of William Wallace, I felt that I must push on. At the end of the route it would be the end of the pain for me. I did not have to face the agony of Wallace's end, and in comparison, I felt I could always manage another few miles. I couldn't come to a halt now; London was so near.

I was far ahead in the timescale. It was only Thursday night, the eighteenth; I had been walking only 15 days and I had reached Luton! There was an unreality to it all. I had covered about 400 miles in total, so averaged 27 a day. Dennis had kept a rough track with the mileometer in the van and said my best was 33, my worst about 25.

If I got some sleep I reckoned I could push on to St Albans, another 12 miles or so, and then we could drive all the way up to Aberdeen for the Friday night and I could go to the Wallace Commemoration there. The day after that, the Saturday, was the Stonehaven Wallace Day, and as all my patriot friends would be there and the bands would be great, I really wanted to go. It was down to Dennis of course. He would have to drive all the way up, then drive back as soon as the Saturday night was over at midnight. I would try to finish the walk into London on the Sunday, the twenty-first, as I was already getting asked to do a lot of media interviews on Monday the twenty-second, the day that Wallace was taken into London.

So I pushed on to St Albans, on the A1081, the A6 having come to a halt at Luton. Every step was absolute pain. It was my blistered feet that were the problem. I had no muscle pain at all. Fluid was building up between my heel bone and the pad and had to come out somewhere, so there were blisters around the edge of my heels, which were getting increasingly bloody.

The last few miles were through gritted teeth, every step.

When I eventually reached St Albans, and the corner of Watling St, I just fell into the van, and we immediately drove on to the M10 then the M1 and headed north. I passed out almost straight away, and we were well on our way back to Scotland when I eventually stirred from my deep sleep.

We reached Aberdeen in time for me to make a speech at the magnificent Wallace statue. It was strange to be awake and not be walking. Strange to just stand on my well-bandaged feet and talk to people. I was very tanned, and my hair had lightened several shades of blonde through being in open air constantly, and everyone commented on how well I looked, but I was absolutely shattered and my mental condition was not good. I was in a strange place with the punishment of it all. Plus, I could not really come to terms with the fact I had walked so far.

Aberdeen was great. I slept in a house that night, and had a great time at Stonehaven the next day, giving a speech in the shadow of Dunnottar Castle. When the evening came to a close at midnight, I slept while Dennis and his non-alcoholic brain drove south.

We diverted slightly into East Kilbride to pick up my daughter, Kimberley, who wanted to walk into London with me. When I woke, Dennis had reached Preston, and I took over to let him sleep and drove till we reached St Albans.

I reckoned it was just over 20 miles to the Thames at Westminster and I felt refreshed with the little break – or so I thought. Kimberley and I set off to finish the journey. We walked along the ancient Roman route of Watling Street, which is today called Edgware Road when it reaches central London.

As we walked, I realised that this was probably the way Wallace was brought on his last stretch too, Watling Street being such an ancient route. A glance at any map (Watling Street's modern designation is the A5) will show how straight it runs. There was a modern church just as we began, strangely named St Bartholomew's. I wondered if I walked in Wallace's very footsteps here, 700 years after the fact.

I thought this last score of miles would be straightforward, but I had underestimated how sore and tired I was. I really struggled. Kimberley was young, fit and carrying no excess, was wearing the right clothing, and I thought she would set a hard pace. It was a bit surprising when she started to struggle, and after ten miles said that the balls of her feet were burning and her hips were sore. Next time we caught up with Dennis she announced that I was stark raving bonkers, and disappeared into the van to let me get on with it.

The last ten miles through London were absolute hell. Especially when I next passed the van and the side door was open and I saw Kimberley lying in my bunk with a big cup of coffee in one hand and a book in the other, oblivious to my suffering. She had managed ten miles at least, which is a lot of walking to your average person, and I hope it let her see what her dad had gone through.

Over the North Circular Road on a footbridge, and on towards the Thames. I was really dragging my feet now. The pavements got more crowded and it was hard in my weak state to avoid passers-by, and Londoners are not especially courteous about giving leeway to anyone coming the other way!

After many hours of slow walking I reached Maida Vale, and carried on till Marble Arch came into view. I passed the site of Tyburn, that other great place of execution in London. The plaque stands in the middle of the road, and I thought of all the poor devils that had been buried beneath the gallows there.

Through the underpass and on down Park Lane. It worked out well that it was a Sunday, as Dennis was able to track me in the van, something that would have been impossible on a weekday when the City of London is usually clogged.

I cut through Green Park, over into St James's Park, and all of a sudden I saw the towers of the Houses of Parliament a half mile or so in front of me. I was so relieved, and in so much pain, I became tearful. I staggered into Parliament Square and out onto Westminster Bridge with the Thames below. I was finished in more ways than one. I was at the sobbing stage now. I walked back a few yards and Dennis and Kimberley picked me up in the van. I was so, so tired and emotional. I couldn't really believe I had done it. Robroyston to the Thames, and I had walked every step of the way. I had actually walked Wallace's last journey.

Was it harder than I expected? That was what most people asked. Yes, it was ten times tougher than I envisaged. But at the same time I did not really think beforehand that I would manage to complete the whole distance. So there is a balance in there somewhere.

Would I do it again? Never in a million years. I am writing this a few weeks on and my feet are still trying to heal. Perhaps in a month or so I will feel the yearning to get out and walk again, but it will be in Scotland, and it will be for enjoyment and at a leisurely pace. I never want my head to get in that state again.

The one bonus was that my old illnesses just seemed to disappear. I had no foot pain other than the blisters, my right foot arch never bothered me, and my heart never missed a beat. It seems somehow, that when a job has to be done, things do fall into place.

CHAPTER ELEVEN

The Commemoration

MONDAY THE TWENTY-SECOND was spent doing interviews for the press and radio, and I appeared on *Good Morning*, a television show, dressed once more in my plaid. The presenter said, 'So are you advocating Home Rule for Scotland?' to which I replied, 'I've actually been a long term advocate for Home Rule for England.' It went straight over his head. That is because the Scots are a sub-servient wee ethnic group somewhere north and when the same terms that are used for us are fired back at them, they just don't get it.

Everyone in Scotland told me that they laughed, and I hope that those who had stuck up the 'Campaign for an English Parliament' stickers I saw had a little laugh too.

TVP, the television crew from Aberdeen who were making a DVD about the whole 700th, met up with me afterwards at Westminster Bridge, and got me to walk back and forwards over the river while they filmed away and did the interview. It poured with rain, some of the heaviest I have ever seen.

While on Westminster Bridge I met a couple who were obviously down for the twenty-third. She was pushing a kilted, bearded man in a wheelchair, and I promised I would try to get them into the church the next day.

Many Scots of my acquaintance were appearing in London now, and much mobile phoning meant that we had all arranged to meet in a pub in Trafalgar Square. Quite a sizeable crowd turned up. I thought this was going to be a good night till I went up to the bar for one spirit and two wee bottles of beer. 'How much?' I could have got a bus to London from Glasgow cheaper! Honestly!

Some folk presented me with a bottle of malt whisky though, and I consoled myself with that. I really should have had an early night, but a group of us ended up walking to Smithfield and standing at the plaque to Wallace's memory at one o'clock in the morning.

I got to my bed about 3AM, then the phone rang at seven, with Radio Scotland asking if they could do an interview. I stood under a cold shower and went out into the rush hour to do the show in the street, relayed back to Scotland by satellite. Just three minutes before we went on air, I saw two black guys approaching, coming up behind the radio people, and I thought they must be with the BBC too. All of a sudden they grabbed some of the equipment and tried to make off with it, in rush hour, in broad daylight! When the presenter tried to stop them, one of them grabbed her mobile phone. At this, I'm afraid I went into primeval mode, and I'm glad it was not live on radio.

Whatever was taken was dropped, and the Radio Scotland girl regained her composure, and her phone, and we went live and did the show. It was a surreal start to the day.

From there we drove over to the church of St Bartholomew the Great at Smithfield. Ted Christopher and Ronnie Browne were there already, so my musicians were in place. Ronnie is a legend to me, and having never met him before, I just sort of kept shaking his hand. He must have thought I was a strange one.

We manhandled the coffin out from under my bunk, and a few of the boys already gathered helped carry it into the church. The people I had chosen as pallbearers turned up and managed to get some practice in. Then it was a mad dash by taxi down to the Houses of Parliament and Westminster Hall. The SNP Members of Parliament had phoned and said they would try and get some of us into Westminster Hall to begin the day. This was amazing news. Would I actually get to stand where Wallace stood on this morning, 700 years ago to the day?

When we pulled up there were many hundreds outside, a mass of tartan and Saltires waving. I could not really believe there were so many people there. It seemed many had already managed to get access to Westminster Hall, and I was hustled through to get inside, as this all revolved around me in some strange way. Gary Stewart, a mate from Glasgow, caught my attention. He had a sword in his hand, its blade in a scabbard, and he threw it to me. I had ordered a new sword from Armour Class in Glasgow and he had picked it up and brought it down to London for me. I also had on a large dirk, which was a present from a Scottish friend based in Canada, Jim Crawford.

You have to go through a security procedure before you get access to Westminster Hall. It is exactly like the ones at airports, with a conveyor belt with a scanner for you to put your bags on, and a sensor doorway to walk through. Police officers stood around.

One of the officers asked me to put any metal objects I had on the conveyor belt. I drew my sword and dirk and placed them on it, then walked through, to smiles and shaking of the officers' heads. I called back to the guys behind me to put their weapons on the belt, and the thirty or so behind me nodded and there was a screek of steel as various weapons were drawn. It seems that every Scot who had come to London for the commemoration had come in kilt or plaid, and was armed to the teeth.

There is no evil intent in this, of course, it is just our way, history being of prime importance in the Celtic soul. All of the guys I know wear weaponry to commemorations in Scotland, and many had asked if they should wear them in London. I was a bit dubious, as it is a foreign country and the authorities might have taken a dim view, and I did not want anyone's day ruined.

In Scotland there have never been problems, as the police understand the pageantry, and that we are not thugs. We want autonomy for our native land, and wearing weapons is done out of respect for tradition and not for any kind of intimidation.

I said to everyone who asked that they would not go out in Estonia or France with their weapons, and England would be no different. But I also knew that this was the 700th anniversary of Wallace's murder and that they would want to wear them out of respect and to make a connection. I told them that they should keep them well under wraps where they could not be drawn, and wait until we had a police presence about us before they were uncovered, when it was obvious to the officers that no threat was intended.

They pulled out their weaponry and placed their swords, dirks, claymores and axes on the belt and casually strolled through, sheathing them again on the other side. One story will stick with me forever. Gary Stewart, who is the wee specky guy holding a burning torch on the cover of my book *A Passion for Scotland*, pulled out his sword and dirk and walked into the sensor doorway. It gave a loud beep and the officers stepped forward to search him, but Gary stepped back, said 'sorry', and reached under his plaid to pull out an old flintlock pistol, adding helpfully, 'I forgot about that one', with no hint of irony, as none was intended, and placed it on the conveyor belt. I heard one officer say to a colleague, 'Christ, they've got guns as well!'

But they knew we meant no harm, and we were allowed to proceed into Westminster Hall, and a crowd gathered round the spot where Wallace stood on his final day. I just stood and looked at the roof and windows of this ancient place and thought of poor Wallace. Could he envisage us here? Would he have thought that so many generations on we would have cared so much? We all love Scotland, just as he did.

God! You could look around and feel the centuries weigh heavily. Quite a crowd had gathered and the SNP Members of Parliament who were present kicked off proceedings.

A few words were said, a quaich of whisky was drunk, 'Freedom Come All Ye' was sung, and a candle, standing on the spot where Wallace had stood, was lit.

I said a few words. Just words that came to me, about Wallace and unfinished business, and most of all, freedom. The crowd began to chant, 'Wallace, Wallace!' and I stood where he had stood and I could not quite believe it. I saw the hall through his eyes. There was electricity in the air and we all felt it. My good friend Matthew Richardson from Canada was in the hall, his bagpipes under his arm. I called him over and asked him to play. He skirled out 'Scots Wha Hae.' People just stared at first, as music is not allowed in Westminster Hall, but I dismissed it by telling them that, 'the pipes have been banned too many times before.'

And they have. This is who we are.

I walked down the hall, the press furiously snapping, and out into the sunlight. We walked out of Westminster Hall, probably through the same door as Wallace had 700 years before.

There was a sea of Saltires flying outside, the sun shining. They were waiting for me to lead them through London, and I was so proud. So proud I could have burst. There was real spirit present, and every face was smiling. There is so much patriotism and love in so many Scots, and they have no outlet for it. They go through their lives wishing – wanting to be able to express what is in their hearts and minds and souls – and the Unionist politicians miss the point completely. But today the ordinary Scots had that chance. That one chance. And I make no apologies. We set off up Whitehall, heading for Trafalgar Square, and looking back it was like a whole army, banners flying, was following me.

We walked Wallace's final route, some six miles of it, past so many historic places, exactly as it is laid out earlier in this book. But it was the reaction of the ordinary Londoner and tourist that I enjoyed. Some looked on confused. What was going on here? A sea of tartan and the pipes playing. But there was no animosity. Office girls smiled, many in heels and tight pencil skirts, and I knew they were being mentally stripped by the brawny boys at my back. Taxi drivers leaned on their horns good-naturedly; bus drivers gave the thumbs up.

This is the way it should be. Scotland and England. Two proud but distinct nations, and a mutual respect.

Everybody seemed to be smiling. English folk constantly asked, 'What's going on?' as we walked towards the Tower of London. The street ahead was like a canyon, with a square of blue sky above. Two jets crossed paths in the middle of this square and their white streams formed a perfect Saltire. I looked up at it as I walked on, and I heard the whole crowd behind me exclaim at it too, pointing it out to their fellows. It was all going so perfectly. The London Police were magnificent, shadowing us but managing to be discreet. Motorcycles blocked junctions for us and I noticed police on cycles and the odd van along the way too, just keeping an eye on us, and letting us get on with what we were there for. Wallace.

One wee Scottish guy in a kilt came out of a building to walk right into this crowd of his kilt wearing, flag bearing countrymen. He had no idea what was happening and was completely jaw-dropped!

I was so used to walking that even with my sore feet I was setting a fast pace, and had to school myself to slow down so the crowd could keep up. In comparison to what I had walked in the previous weeks, the six miles or so through London were a mere stroll, so I was amused when I later heard folk complain about their blistered feet after such a short walk. Well, short to me now, but I did say earlier that the first time I walked four miles I was pleased with myself.

As we turned into Smithfield I could see that there were already many people gathered there and the monument to Wallace's memory was bedecked with flowers.

I said a few words. Scott Begbie, a reporter from the Aberdeen area, said a few words. And *Clann an Drumma*, with their primeval brand of pipe and drums, let rip and fired up the crowd.

But the real roller coaster of emotion had yet to come.

I made my way over to the door of St Bartholomew the Great, and with the aid of some of the boys from *Siol nan Gaidheal*, checked that those filing in had invitations. As I had sent all these out over the last year or so to those who had asked or enquired early enough, I knew nearly every address or location, and was able to vet those passing through.

I spotted Willie Wolfe, an old stalwart of the SNP, wandering around Smithfield, and rushed over to ask if he wanted to come in. Old as he was, and I mean no disrespect in that, he had made his way down from Scotland just to be there. I ushered him because he deserved to be inside.

I must say that I am first and foremost a patriot, and not really a political animal, but the SNP were the only party to really help on the day, as you would probably have expected. There is no use in preaching only to the converted, I'm sure you will all agree, and if politicians from other persuasions had wanted to take part I would have invited them with open arms, in the hope that they would have realised that announcing your Scottishness is no shame.

The woman with the guy in the wheelchair that I met on Westminster Bridge turned up, and of course, I ushered them through. All those with invites filtered through, and although the service did not start till 3PM, by about twenty to, the church was full. There were a few chancers trying to bluff their way in – one woman in particular – but there was no special pecking order in getting an invite in the first place. You only needed to get in touch with me and ask, email being the usual method. Folk would ask for an invite, I would email them back and ask them to put their thoughts on Wallace down for me, and tell me why they thought they should be there, and I judged it by their answers.

One reply said, 'I can't put my thoughts on Wallace down. It is too deeply embedded in my soul and I would not know where to start.' That person got one.

I got queries from all over the planet, almost all from ex-pat Scots or those of Scottish descent. I did my best to include a good sized group of these people, as in the 700 years since Wallace's time we have spread over the face of the Earth, and I wanted to reflect that.

I was about the last to walk into the church, and what hit me was the absolute silence. It was deafening. St Bartholomew the Great is a striking, old and very beautiful church. You can sense the very age of its gnarled grey stonework. Everyone was sitting, gazing up at the wooden-raftered roof and towering stone walls, or looking to their feet in contemplation. As they walked into that ancient interior, I think the hard reality hit them all. It was the 700th anniversary to the day, and they were in the building that was probably the last thing that Wallace saw. He was torn to pieces as the opening spectacle of St Bartholomew's Fair exactly seven centuries before.

All I could hear was the tap of my little leather brogans on the stone floor. There was a chair with my name on it just to the side of the lectern where the speeches were to be made. I sat down, and gazed across at the choir stalls where the London Gaelic Choir was sitting. The whole church sat in silence, till on the stroke of three, Dr Dudley, the rector of St Bartholomew's, and Reverend Alan Sorensen, my well-chosen Church of Scotland minister, made their welcomes and introductions.

At that, the tenor of the choir sang 'Scots Wha Hae', the doors opened, and the pallbearers bore the coffin into the church, draped in the Saltire. The Saltire pall-cloth had been made by Smiler, a friend from the Isle of Lewis. A labour of love, fringed and tasseled. I watched as it was carried down that central aisle, with all the seating facing into the centre of the church, and I saw how every eye stared straight at that coffin.

The pipes played and the coffin was placed on trestles at the end of the aisle. Hymns were sung, then Dr Fiona Watson of Stirling University rose to speak. She gave her reflections on the life of Wallace. I was glad Fiona had accepted and agreed to be the first speaker. It was nice to have a female perspective where Wallace was concerned, as I think he is often seen as such a macho figure. I admire Fiona. She is very much the academic, but manages to speak unselfconsciously and with more passion than she knows.

If anyone thought that it was going to be a straightforward funeral-style service, this illusion was soon dispelled when Ted Christopher was introduced and sang his specially written song 'I'm Coming Home.' He walked down the aisle as he played and the first lines echoed through the ancient building, 'I did not close my eyes for the last time under Caledonian skies, with my good friends gathered all around me to say their last goodbyes…'

I knew every eye was beginning to fill. There was an electricity, a magic in the air, and although people round about me were beginning to openly cry, I knew that every one of them was brimming with pride and was so glad they were there.

Alex Salmond, the leader of the Scottish National Party, was the next to speak. His opening words were, 'There is nowhere in the world I would rather be today…' and he gave a stirring speech about Wallace, Scotland, and where Scotland is going. It was well received. Sometimes you know when you are alive – really, really alive – and we all knew it that day in the church of St Bartholomew the Great.

Ronnie Browne. A legend. He stood to sing 'Flower of Scotland.' Just to hear that voice that we all knew so well echo round that ancient church! Ronnie stood at the side of the coffin, but he hesitated. We knew he was overcome with emotion. We all were. Someone called out, 'We'll help you Ronnie!' and he began, a little falteringly, but of course every mouth began to quietly sing along with him, and Ronnie, seasoned performer, put his heart and soul into it. What a moment! I would have given a fortune to have seen that alone. And I heard many a female say that Ronnie was 'sex on legs'. Must be something in the Scottish water that makes us menfolk ripen with age. Women seem to swoon at the likes of Ronnie and Sean Connery.

Then I knew it was my turn. My friend Marshall, one of the *Guarde Ecosse*, had given me a small pouch at Dunnottar a few days before with a little soil in it. I added a little more, and as Marshall and I chatted that day he spoke of the very soil of Scotland and gave me the basis for what I wanted to say in St Bartholomew's.

I can't remember it all, as I always just open my mouth and see what comes out. I've never really prepared a speech, but I usually have a rough framework inside my head. But the rough gist of it was that I opened with the line, 'As long as a hundred of us remain alive', and opened my arms to encompass all in that church. They all understood that of course. I took the little bag from my sporran and scattered some of the soil on the floor. I explained that it was the soil of Scotland, the very soil from which we spring, the soil that we grow on. Our soil. And when we die we go back to that soil, and our very ashes form the nation itself. We all, and the soil of Scotland, are one and the same, indivisible. And if I happened to die abroad, I begged them to never let a corner of a foreign field be forever Scotland. I wanted to come home.

Then I spoke of Wallace and how he had died abroad, and most of his atoms were scattered, and how he must yearn to come home to his own. And we were there that day to take his spirit back to the country he loved. He died facing that church in which we had gathered. Did not some shade of him flee to this sanctuary as his heart was torn from him, ending his life?

I asked if they could sense him there. I could. I explained how in life we all have doubts. We doubt our convictions, our patriotism, our beliefs, our politics at times. But if I ever have doubts where Scotland is concerned, one name is always there to set me on the straight and narrow. William Wallace.

I managed to get through it, voice cracking once or twice. I had feared I would stand and look between all those faces of my fellows, down that aisle, to that coffin draped in the Saltire, and not be able to do it. But I got through. I had to, really.

The Reverend Sorensen gave a moving and stirring sermon. He described Jesus being tortured on the cross, how there was nothing but hatred all around, the faces contorted with hate and loathing. None of the similarities were lost on us. He was brilliant. Everyone remarked on his ability afterwards.

Dr Dudley, the Rector of St Bartholomew's, gave us words of welcome and ended with a blessing. There is a religious gap between the faiths of these two churchmen, but they worked together brilliantly on the day, to turn it into a deeply spiritual and moving occasion.

The coffin was then undraped and opened. People had brought little mementos to place inside. They lined up, not a word spoken, and waited their turn to drop their memento in. At this point, the *Coisir Lunnainn*, the London Gaelic Choir, sang several songs. It was electric. Those amazing voices singing in the old tongue of Scotland, the rising notes in perfect harmonies filling that ancient building, an echo across the centuries. The faces were a study. Many ashen, many pallid, and all struggling with their emotions.

As they stepped up to the coffin, I saw people kiss their mementos and pat the casket, before making their way back to their seats.

I saw a woman push a wheelchair up the aisle – the couple I had met on Westminster Bridge. Some of the pallbearers stepped forward to assist, but the man in the wheelchair waved them back. He was frail in body, but determined. His arms shook as he attempted to stand. He pushed himself up, shaking, just far enough to throw his token the last foot or two, and it landed within the coffin. He fell back exhausted, but obviously happy that he had made his connection with Wallace. I saw the tears fall from the faces of some hard men as they watched this.

Eventually, all had returned to their seats. Nearly all sat, heads bowed, as the sound of the choir continued for several minutes. They were deep in thought. I knew there was a deep love of Scotland inside them all, and here there was an opportunity for that love to come straight to the surface. A love that the politicians don't really seem to understand, or have the ability to harness. And it is an awesome power when it is unleashed. Primeval, unquestioning love for the scrap of land that our ancestors colonised so that we could call it our own. It was what Wallace and his army fought for at Stirling Bridge.

The last prayer was sung, the Benediction was given by Dr Dudley, the coffin was closed and the Saltire pall-cloth draped over it. The pallbearers shouldered the weight, the coffin lifted from its trestles, and to 'Lord Lovat's Lament', played by Jim Gee, the pallbearers slow-marched through the church and out to the sunshine.

Everyone told me later that as they watched the coffin go down the aisle, they believed, they really believed, that Wallace was inside.

I had seen a momentous occasion take place; a day I would remember forever. You can say to most people, 'Tell me something you did at the age of, say, 33', and unless something momentous happened that year, they will be unable to answer with any real surety. But ask any single person in that church in the future if they can remember something from 2005, and they will recall that day vividly. 'One of the best days of my life' was a line I heard again and again.

As we walked out of the church a pipe band was formed up. It was the Alaska Highlanders, all the way from – you guessed it – Alaska! They had emailed me a few times and said that they wished to turn up just to do their own musical tribute to Wallace. I was not sure they would turn up, as the logistics of the exercise were huge, but turn up they did. The march set off, flanked by police motor-cycles and with mounted policemen leading, with the Alaska Highlanders Pipe Band showing the way. The police were superb. It was now about 4.45PM, so it was rush hour in London, and they stopped the traffic for us at every junction and let us march unhindered.

What your average Londoner made of this lot was anyone's guess. A pipe band followed by pallbearers carrying a coffin draped in the Saltire, followed by several hundred mourners dressed in tartan, almost all of them armed with swords, and a plethora of Saltires held aloft.

We marched down Holborn, and onto Grays Inn Road. The chant of 'Wallace! Wallace!' went up, and continued. We reached the scene of the evening event, the Welsh Centre, the home of Welsh people in London. Everyone invited had kept their order of service, so we were quickly able to check who was supposed to be there as an invited guest.

The coffin was carried in and placed on the front of the stage. Prince Michael spoke to the crowd about what a day it had been, and then various pipers gave it their best shot to outdo one another. One girl – about 20 years of age – in a long dress – Judy – blew the place apart with her ability, and jaw-dropped quite a few of us!

A nice touch was that Mhairi Calvey, the girl who played the young Murron in *Braveheart*, now 16, was there, and happily posed for pictures with the guys. A wee bit of Hollywood! And she looked great in her black dress. She said she was so honoured to have been there, and we were honoured to have her presence, a part of the continuing story of Wallace.

The Alaska Highlanders played in the hall, and then the stage was given over to *Clann an Drumma*, who had the whole hall going wild, the Saltires still waving among the crowd. Ted Christopher was joined by his band, Bannockburn, and they played on for the rest of the evening, the hall a sea of dancing bodies, their emotions let loose after the pathos of the day.

In the middle of this I was given a surprise presentation by the Society of William Wallace, crafted by the lady who had done so much to help put the London events in place, Sheila MacLean. It was a creation of stained glass, which lit up, and the front-piece was a picture of myself and Sir William Wallace, both of us grasping the same sword. It bears the lines told to Wallace in his youth, spoken by his uncle:

'Freedom is best, I tell thee true, of all things to be won, then never live within the bonds of slavery my son.'

Words fail me at such times. I am not really good at accepting praise or gifts; never have been. But it was much appreciated.

At the evening's end, Ted again sang 'I'm Coming Home' and the boys lifted the coffin aloft and bore it from the hall, back into the van. Dennis and I were to take it north to Scotland the next morning. We had done it. For 700 years, until now, nothing had been done to commemorate Wallace, to bring his spirit home.

The next day every paper in Scotland carried the story, with pictures, and even then the familiar Scottish cringe was firmly in place. *The Scotsman*, for example, said 'about 100 Scottish patriots gathered in London...' 100? Over 1,000 was the truth, with 300 in the church alone. Any why 'Scottish' patriots? Surely a Scottish newspaper should just have used the word 'patriots.'

Some papers said that we had remembered 'the rebel Wallace'. Rebel? How can a Scot fighting for Scotland be a rebel?

But we had extensive news coverage in Scotland, and that was a good thing. Folk who cared could sit in their armchairs and see that there were others who cared too, and that they were not alone.

I was exhausted, physically and emotionally. I had walked to London, and had done countless media interviews since I had arrived, and given many speeches, most memorably at Westminster Hall, Smithfield, St Bartholomew the Great, and at the evening event at the Welsh Centre.

But if I am going to have a better day in my life than that spent on 23 August 2005, it will have to be something very, very special.

I had seen something. The true spirit of Scotland. An open armed, smiling, expansive, truthful and whole-hearted goodness, a spiritual patriotism that had everyone grasping each other as true brothers and sisters. This was so far removed from the grim faced and resentful Unionism that I unfortunately see within Scottish society; that narrow minded and conservative stance that shackles the freedom of my country.

And Sir William Wallace?

I hope you looked down William, and smiled.

CHAPTER TWELVE

I'm Coming Home

SOME SNP MEMBERS OF PARLIAMENT that had been present asked me, 'How can we bottle that emotion, that true spirit of Scotland that we saw?' I'm not sure of the answer, but I know now that there is a sense of history and a caring about where we are going within the Scots people that just needs a catalyst to release it.

The next morning many of us grasped hands and knew that we would all meet again at events to come in Scotland.

Driving home with Dennis, his lady, Shona, and my daughter Kimberley in the van, along with the Spirit of Wallace in the back, I marveled at the distance I had covered on foot, as the drive seemed to take forever.

I had told a few folk that we would stop at Gretna on the border, just to take the coffin out of the van for a few minutes.

As we took the exit at the beginning of the M74 and came up to the lay-by on the left, just by 'The First House in Scotland', I saw some Saltires flying, come to wish the Spirit of Wallace home. Helping hands took the coffin out, and we carried it a few feet to the top of a little rise, from which point we could see across the Solway to where Longshanks had breathed his last.

It was a moment of mixed emotions; pleasure at coming home, tinged with the view of the place where the man who had murdered Wallace had departed this life.

I decided we should unscrew the coffin lid, to let the air of Scotland enter it. We undid the four handles that kept the lid in place, and eased it off. No one had seen inside of course, as the coffin had been sitting at about head height on the trestles in the church.

We gathered round and just stared. It was pretty much full. Notes, flowers, miniature bottles of whisky, little things that people had made, like embroidery or carved pieces of wood, a whole jumble of keepsakes and mementos. I spotted a flag that had been put in by a yachtsman I knew, who had circumnavigated most of the planet. He flew a special red ensign – with the Saltire in one quarter – from his boat, and had placed it in the coffin. Many little things that had a special relevance to the people concerned. We did not really want to touch anything, and after a few minutes the lid was replaced. Again, we were very emotional, the genuine goodness of our countryfolk having touched us all.

He was home.

Back into the van, and we carried on north. The next day the coffin was taken to the Stirling Smith Art Gallery and Museum, where it went into the keeping of Elspeth King, the curator, who had built the most amazing catafalque to take it. It was like a medieval saint's shrine, roofed and surrounded by candles, its sides decorated with paintings of Scottish saints.

The boys from *Clann an Drumma* turned up, as did Ted Christopher, everyone now determined to see this thing through. Most of the pallbearers managed to make it, so we knew we could give the Spirit of Wallace a decent return to Stirling, the scene of his great victory.

The Provost of Stirling, Colin O'Brien, was there with Elspeth as a wee welcoming committee. A decent crowd had gathered too. *Clann an Drumma* played on the steps, and at exactly midday on 25 August the pallbearers walked round the corner of the Smith to carry the coffin home. It was slid into the catafalque and Ted again sang 'I'm Coming Home.' Again I could see the emotion on every face.

Clann an Drumma played another couple of songs by the coffin, then we left the Spirit of Wallace to lie for a few weeks where people could visit it and leave their messages. It looked amazing sitting there, in the middle of an exhibition of Wallace artefacts, like the lying in state of a great leader.

And it was. It was the dignity that Wallace was denied in 1305.

On 10 September we again arrived at the Smith, this time to take the coffin to Lanark for the 'Homecoming'. This was to be the return of Wallace to the town where, it is hoped, he spent his happiest moments, legend stating that he met Marion and married her in Lanark at St Kentigern's. No matter what, this was the place where it all began, Wallace slaying Heselrig, the English sheriff here, and kicking off the first stage of the fight back against English occupation.

Heselrig would have been in the castle, and Wallace would have stormed in, helped by the townsfolk of Lanark. The castle site is now home to the bowling greens beside Castlebank Park. The greens stand atop a defensive hilltop, traces of earthworks still clearly visible. A plaque at the entrance has been renewed, telling how parliaments were once held here.

It's strange to watch a quiet game of bowls here on a summer's day, knowing that the Scots once stormed the place, Wallace in the lead, to kill Heselrig and rid the town of invaders.

Incidentally, you may wish to know the origins of Heselrig. His full name, William de Heselrig, just means William of Heselrig. The place in question is today called Hazelrigg, in Chatton, Northumberland, a few miles from Heaton on the River Till.

I got a call from Baron Lee, an American gentleman who had bought Lee Castle estate, a little to the north of Lanark. This venerable pile was once the home of the Lockheart family, of ancient stock, originally called Loccard, their name changed slightly as they supplied the casket that held the heart of the Bruce, taken on crusade by the Black Douglas.

The Baron informed me that he had a chapel within the castle walls where the coffin could lie till the commemorations took place in Lanark the following day.

So on the afternoon of Saturday September 10, a little cavalcade of vehicles meandered down the hilly drive to Lee Castle. The pallbearers had arrived to carry the coffin in with the dignity it deserved.

Lee Castle is an impressive pile and the Baron had been good enough to deck the chapel out with flowers and candles. The coffin was placed at the altar to lie overnight, and the candles lit. I took a last look at it there, draped in its Saltire, beams of light coming through the stained glass, the lit candles almost like companions to see it through the hours of darkness.

The following morning, Sunday 11 September, the 708th anniversary of the battle of Stirling Bridge, and the eighth since the day of the Yes/Yes vote to reconvene the Scottish Parliament, we held a little service in the chapel. Prince Michael was there, the Baron and a few friends were there, and my pallbearers were there. At the end of it I told them I knew that we all now had an emotional attachment to the coffin, that we would do our best that day in Lanark and that we would do our best for Scotland.

Scotland. It's all I ever had. We would carry out that day with dignity. We would carry the Spirit of Wallace back to Lanark with all the pathos we could muster. It was only a wee thing, but it was a chance to again unleash that spirit we had seen in London. A good, wholesome, open-armed patriotism. To let some of the people of Scotland feel it in their very core. That was all I ever wanted.

The coffin was taken to the south gatehouse of the Lee Estate, and from there we bore it towards the town, the *Guarde Ecosse* flanking the pallbearers, Dennis and I leading, swords drawn. We crossed the bridge over the Mouse Water and into the environs of Lanark itself.

At the Cartland Bridge Hotel many hundreds were gathered to parade the coffin into the town. The Society of William Wallace was well represented, the Society's large banner in evidence. So many faces I knew well. So many patriot hearts. The true voice of Scotland. I may have been a catalyst, but this was all about the Scottish people. Every facet of this, from planning the London event, through to this final chapter, was about people. It would not have – could not have – happened if it was not in the will of the people who supported me.

If I used William Wallace in any of this, I'm sure he would have understood, perhaps even approved.

Pipes playing, we set off for the middle of the town, the coffin now on a cart, and a plucky little horse pulling it on.

We gathered at the Wallace House site, where the coffin was borne into a medieval style tent. Legend states that this is where the house that was involved in the very start of the events that led up to Wallace's uprising against foreign occupation once stood.

It is reputed to be the site of Marion's family's town house (they were wealthy, having their main seat at Lamington, further upstream on the Clyde, and this was their town property, such as many wealthy families had).

Wallace is said to have got into a fracas with some English soldiers, which resulted in a careless Englishman losing his hand to a sweep of Wallace's sword. Marion, watching from a window, opened the front door for Wallace to escape through the house to safety. This resulted in a furious Heselrig having her slain. The rest is history, or at least legend. No matter, it is important that this house site exists.

There was a plain plaque here originally, as sketched in my *On the Trail of William Wallace* book, but a new plaque was unveiled at this ceremony, featuring both William and Marion – a nice touch. Andy Hillhouse, who supplied the artwork for the tickets to the Commemoration, provided the artistry for the plaque.

Speeches were made, and I was a little surprised at the size of the crowd that had gathered. Again, Saltires were flying, and there was that certain Scots something in the air.

Speeches over, and people queued to see the coffin. The Lanark Wallace Heritage Trust, which had ordered the day's proceedings, had placed a box for messages in the tent, and left a guest book for folk to sign and write their thoughts.

The queue was huge, and as I stood by the coffin with the other pallbearers, I could not believe how calm and courteous those queuing were, and how long they were prepared to wait. And the flowers! The coffin, after a few minutes, was covered in floral tributes. Some of the wreaths must have cost a small fortune.

The coffin sat at the house site for most of the afternoon, and a wee group of us from the Society of William Wallace and *Siol nan Gaidheal* took turns to answer questions and just generally be present, whilst others nipped round the corner to the aptly named Wallace Cave pub for food and refreshment.

There used to be a stream that ran down Lanark's Main Street, but it was tunneled in many, many years ago. It runs under the Wallace Cave pub and there are tales that Wallace used the old cave through which the stream ran as an escape route, so it was a place that had a connection to the day's proceedings.

The coffin was later put on the cart and pulled by Dougal the sturdy horse, and the procession made its way down to Castlebank Park, adjacent to the castle site where Wallace slew Heselrig.

It was difficult to grasp the enormity of all this at the time. Still is, to be honest. We had brought the Spirit of Wallace back from London. We had brought the coffin back to the very place where his career began, here at the castle in Lanark. What would Wallace have made of it all?

The coffin was laid on trestles right at the front of the stage that had been erected for the day's events. The guys stood around the coffin, and a large crowd gathered behind them. I had previously joked with the Lanark William Wallace Heritage Trust that I could guarantee them no rain. I told them I had signed a deal with God and that it never rained on the important events that I arranged. Never usually did, either. It was a gorgeous day, yet the day before had been wet. I got up on the stage to announce that Ronnie Browne and Ted Christopher would be singing shortly, and said a few words to the crowd. As I did this, I watched two jets in the sky cross paths, their vapour trails forming a perfect Saltire behind the crowd. The same had happened while we walked through London. Perhaps Wallace did approve after all.

Ken Shirra of the Scottish Knights Templar gave two very good speeches that day, one at the house earlier, and one here where the coffin was blessed.

Once Ted had again sung 'I'm Coming Home' – and this time the crowd were beginning to know it well enough to sing along – and Ronnie had sung 'Flower of Scotland', both to an ecstatic audience, the coffin was again lifted on to the cart, to await its final journey up through the town, on a route that Wallace himself must have walked many times, to St Kentigern's Church.

Dusk was gathering as the procession set off. Uphill again to the Wallace house site, then on to the church.

The coffin was laid down at the church entrance, and I watched the procession come on at our backs. And on. And on. I couldn't believe the number of people who had gathered. There was a sea of faces outside the church, and still they came up the street.

I gave a little speech. Again I explained how the blood from Stirling Bridge and Falkirk had not gone anywhere. How it ran in all our veins. All Scots together. And all the true Lanarkians in the crowd would have the blood of those who had followed Wallace on that fateful night when Heselrig was slain running in their veins.

It was a daunting thought really. These people who stood here seven centuries after the event were in fact part of what had happened.

A monk appeared, representing John Blair, Wallace's personal chaplain. Six other monks, their faces hidden by their cowls, accompanied him. A young girl was with them, representing Marion, come to welcome William Wallace home. I was meant to narrate all this, and did my best, but the girl's face was tear-stained as she reached the coffin, and I knew the words were going to stick in my throat. She threw herself upon the coffin, racked with sobs. She was a local actress, but I think the enormity of what she was doing took her by surprise. The Spirit of Wallace himself was before her, and the tears were real.

The coffin was lifted, and Marion and the monks carried it on into the church. Although the sky was darkening into night, I looked up again to see two more vapour trails forming a Saltire above the church. This was becoming a little uncanny. People were pointing upwards and cameras were flashing.

Skirlie, a piper from Stonehaven, who had blown lustily on the streets of London, stood upon a floodlit gantry as the coffin was carried up towards the church, flames guiding the route at either side. As the coffin and its attendants passed, the flames went out. A great bit of carefully rehearsed showcasing. As Skirlie finished, I asked the crowd for a minute's silence in respect of Wallace's home-coming. You could have heard a pin drop. Not a sound in that crowd of thousands.

At the end of the silence, a sonic bomb was detonated within the church like a thunderclap and the whole building lit up red, the glow lighting the night sky. Wallace was home.

The monks reappeared, carrying swords. These were thrust into a brazier, which burst into flame. Torches were lit, and they lit others, till there was a sea of flame lighting the crowd.

They then headed back down through the town to Castlebank Park, and it was amazing to see that crowd, a mass of burning torches dictating its route, go downhill between the houses of the town, twisting and turning snake-like, a sea of humanity carrying out homage to their national hero. Saltires carried high.

At Castlebank, musicians played, and the best fireworks display I had ever seen lit the night sky. Lanark had done Wallace proud. I could not really believe I had been responsible for all this. I had needed to do something to unleash the passion I had inside me for my country, and my desire to see it stand independent and proud.

What made it special was the fact that it unleashed so much passion within all those that it touched – a focus for their own sense of Scottishness.

And Wallace looked down and smiled.

At the very last television interview I did that night – in the Wallace Cave, before I left for home – I was asked what I thought I had achieved. I replied, '700 years ago, the people of England tried to extinguish the flame that was William Wallace. I would like to think that seven centuries on, all of us working together have ensured that the flame burns brighter than ever.'

Retrospective

THE EVENTS OF AUGUST 2005 are almost a blur to me. There is an unreality about the proceedings, and I can't really take on board that no one had held any kind of closure for William Wallace for the seven centuries before me.

I knew that I was putting my head in the firing line by doing what I did. But if I did not go ahead and do it, who would?

It was my name that was in the headlines and on the television news, but everyone who knows me well will know that I do not seek anything for myself from my work. I want to see my nation free of foreign rule and that is paramount to me. Much of what happened was paid for out of my own pocket, and I have no problem with that. It needed to be done. But at the end of the day it is people who make projects successful, and people wanted to take part, and so it worked.

Because of the commemoration I was asked to several talk shows and functions and the like. I did a talk show on BBC Scotland, where Nicky Campbell, the host, approached me and said something along the lines of, 'You are a great advocate of anti-English heroes like Wallace and Bruce.'

This is the Scottish self-loathing at its worst. The famous Scottish cringe.

Wallace and Bruce are not and never were anti-English. They stood up for the defence of their nation and the freedom of its people when their country's very existence was under threat. The fact that the aggressor was England was immaterial.

This is not Nicky's fault alone. This is the result of years of indoctrination by a media that is not based in Scotland. If an Englishman said that he was an admirer of Nelson, you would not immediately retort, 'So you hate the French then?' Or if an American stated that he admired Washington you would not suddenly assume that he hated the English.

Yet this happens with Scots, and other Scots usually do it.

At one point in the dialogue of the programme, a girl in the audience spoke of the Scots' wish for independence, and that half of the population desired this. The young man beside her, Ross, I remember his name was, stated that, 'The support for the SNP is only at 20%.'

So he thinks that only those wanting independence vote SNP and that Labour voters are all happy with Unionism?

People in Scotland do not vote Tory as they are seen to be blatantly aligned with Unionism.

I believe that many who vote Labour believe in independence for their nation, but vote Labour for the socialist principles that generations of Scots associate with that party. But the Labour Party in Scotland need to start alienating themselves from England in order to stop this country being asset stripped any further. To them I say, 'Have the bravery and the fire in your soul to create change.'

Just as the events of 2005 finished, the documentation was released that proved that the government in London was ready to use force if necessary to ensure that the Scots did not go their own way when oil was discovered in Scottish waters.

They would have invaded and taken whatever steps were needed to take our natural assets!

For God's sake Scotland. Wake up!

What has to be done to us to get us to see the light?

I was invited to a 'Wallace' commemoration at Stirling Castle shortly after my return from London. Jack McConnell, Scotland's First Minister, hosted it. A gentleman took the stage, playing Wallace perfectly. He berated those present for not pursuing their country's freedom, and I could see that these outrageous claims were a bit close to the knuckle for many present!

But what confused me was the footage of Mel Gibson that appeared on a screen, saying that a great thing had been done in Scotland, as we had finally given Wallace a funeral. I somehow got the impression that he thought that the government of Scotland was responsible for this.

We need the spirit of Wallace in Scotland. We need that spirit to pervade every facet of our establishment.

The Lion of Scotland needs to sharpen its claws, and we need politicians who will stand up for not just the rights of Scotland, but for what is right for Scotland.

We need leaders, leaders that can destroy the Scottish cringe once and for all, and make people proud and make Scots equal on a world stage with every other nation.

We are a sad and sorry little country, dependent on the hand-outs of our masters. And worst of all, both leaders and the ordinary people seem happy to be treated as such.

We need those in charge who are not afraid of change for the better – for a Scotland that is not fighting in illegal wars with peoples with whom she has no personal animosity, and is in charge of her own resources, immigration, banking and welfare – to name but a few of the rights we should all have.

After the Wallace commemorations were over, the Scottish Parliament held several events to mark the anniversary of the Battle of Trafalgar. Yes, the one where Nelson stated that, 'England expects every Englishman to do his duty!' although many of those fighting in that encounter were Scots. Yet nothing had really been done officially to commemorate our National Hero.

Wallace still seems to pose a threat.

I only want what is the right thing for Scotland and no more. The chance to stand as an equal with the other people of this planet, and to see my country's flag fly outside the United Nations and the European Parliament. I say to the leaders of Scotland, is that too much to ask?

One wee word sums it up. It has become synonymous with Wallace. It does not need dressing up in fancy clothes, and all our leaders and politicians should say it without shame.

And that word is Freedom.

The following article was printed in the Glasgow *Herald*, Monday 9 April 1956. It seems that 'Scots Wha Hae' has always been seen as a song of insurrection!

About 100 Scots gathered at the unveiling of a memorial to Sir William Wallace erected on the wall of St Bartholomew's Hospital close to the site of his execution. After the ceremony those present sang the National Anthem. Suddenly a man jumped onto the platform, grabbed the microphone, and shouted, 'Refuse to sing this song!' [Note – this of course refers to 'God save the Queen']

The platform party included the Earl of Dundee, the hereditary Standard Bearer for Scotland, and his Countess. The MP for Kelvin Grove, Mr Walter Elliot, had just given an address. Mr Elliot seized the man, who was then escorted from the platform as he continued to shout. He was taken to Snow Hill Police Station where he was charged with 'insulting behaviour'. The man was later released on a bail of £2 pending trial. His name was given as Padruig MacGillefhinnein, aged 33, chairman of the London Branch of the Scottish National Party.

An unofficial part of the ceremony involved the laying of a wreath by the London Branch of the SNP. A spokesman for the party said that the man's actions were in no way sanctioned by the branch although they did believe that 'Scots Wha Hae' and not the National Anthem should have been sung at the official ceremony. 'Scots Wha Hae' had in fact been sung earlier by the crowd of Scottish spectators.

The Saltire and Lion Rampant were placed over the memorial plaque, but when the time came for the unveiling by the Countess of Dundee the flags refused to part when the ropes were pulled. She tugged again at the ropes but the covering would still not fall away. The Rev Robert V.F. Scott, minister of St Columba's Church of Scotland, Pont Street, and Chairman of the Memorial Committee, stepped forward to help by pulling on the ropes several times. Still nothing happened. Pipe Major Willie Ross played 'The Flowers of the Forest' as the struggle with the ropes continued. Finally the flags covering the memorial had to be simply pulled aside by hand. Reveille was then sounded by two buglers of the Scots Guards.

The memorial consists of a plaque made of Creetown granite. The work was carried out by Edinburgh artist Miss Diana Atchison and part of the inscription declares–

'His example of heroism and devotion inspired those who came after him to win victory from defeat and his memory remains for all time a source of pride, honour and inspiration to his countrymen.'

London Scots raised £1,000 to pay for the memorial and its maintenance. Contributions were also received from Englishmen.

Contents of the coffin made for William Wallace, displayed at the Wallace 700 Exhibition at the Stirling Smith Art Gallery and Museum, Stirling

JEWELLERY
1. One bead necklace.
2. One metal pendant.
3. Medal inscribed, Royal Burgh of Lanark, Laminar Day, 2005.
4. William Wallace badge – Smith Museum.
5. Badge – heart shaped – metal.
6. Medal – showing the Saltire, thistle, and Lion Rampant attached to a tartan ribbon.
7. Saltire brooch – hallmarked silver.
8. One boxed Wallace clan brooch.
9. One glass ladybird (red) pebble.
10. Two small Celtic pill boxes containing soil.
11. One small wooden engraved elephant keyring marked from Thailand.
12. One Highland fashioned metal brooch inlaid with lilac stones.
13. One plastic and metal pin with Gaelic inscription.
14. One pink glass pebble showing the shape of the Saltire inside.
15. One hand-rubbed pebble – beige and black.
16. One painted gold coloured pebble.
17. One black and grey shiny pebble.
18. One coloured photograph of the William Wallace statue at Dryburgh affixed onto a frame.
19. One amulet (shaped like an axe) on a leather string.
20. One thistle-shaped metal pin.
21. One wooden box inlaid with mother-of-pearl. Empty inside.
22. One silk heather lapel brooch.
23. One silk heather lapel brooch with thistles.
24. One silk heather lapel brooch with tartan ribbon.
25. One small black heart-shaped shiny pebble in a small cotton bag.
26. Bouquet of synthetic and silk Scottish thistles wrapped in gauze and tied with a tartan ribbon.
27. One metal pendant on chain with naked lady charm attached (affixed onto the outside handle of the coffin).
28. One metal badge showing the Saltire.
29. One small piece of plaid with pin showing Kircaldy Tartan Army insignia.

RELIGIOUS
1. Small wooden cross with pewter Celtic-shaped cross at centre labelled 'On behalf of the People of the Scottish Borders'.
2. Metal Celtic cross on chain necklace.
3. One metal cross pin and one WW pin affixed onto heather.

4. One metal badge depicting the face of Jesus Christ.
5. One religious medal St John Ogilvie.
6. One set of peace rosary beads – white, in box.
7. Three prayer cards.
8. One set of prayer beads with silver cross attached (on the outside handle of the coffin).
9. Two tartan cards with prayer inlay.

FLAGS
1. Four cloth Saltires unsigned.
2. One cloth Saltire signed by GP Masson.
3. One cloth Saltire signed by J&D&K Liddell.
4. One cloth Saltire showing the Lion Rampant signed W&J&H&C&M McInnes, S&A&A&B&A MacDonald.
5. One small paper Saltire signed J Crawford.
6. One small paper Saltire unsigned.
7. One cloth yacht flag showing the Saltire in the corner, signed D Thomson.
8. One cloth Wallace ceremonial flag, unsigned.

SCARVES
1. One woven Scottish football scarf.
2. One Celtic motif silk scarf.

TIES
1. One tie – MacNaughton tartan.

MISCELLANEOUS
1. One fridge magnet depicting the present Scottish Parliament.
2. One 1992 Canadian Dollar coin.
3. One Clan McKenzie small drinks mat.
4. One small, glass, hanging ornament with Wallace inscribed.
5. One tartan beer mat with a photograph of a Mr and Mrs Stewart attached.
6. Threads of plaid worn by David R. Ross throughout 2005 wrapped around a piece of card (700 threads of colour woven by Christine MacLeod in the Weaver's Cottage Kilbarchan).
7. One wee tartan bag filled with soil.
8. One small tube filled with soil and marked 'From His Homeland'.
9. One tartan hanky containing a pebble.
10. One stone carved with the initials E&R.
11. One small boxed Wallace whisky bottle.
12. One tartan square envelope containing a thistle.
13. One small black velvet bag containing soil.
14. One plastic flower – Scottish white rose.
15. One small beer mat – Clan Menzies.
16. Three feathers.
17. CD – 'I'm Coming Home' by Ted Christopher.
18. One small drinks mat – the Scottish Parliament.

19. Two trade business cards.
20. One paper scroll with writing, wrapped in a small Saltire secured by a tartan ribbon and heather.
21. One small, blue, lidded Tupperware box containing soil.
22. One black armband with tartan inset.
23. One bonnie wee cushion embroidered with the Lion Rampant and signed I Hamilton from Moray.
24. One tartan hanky.
25. One blue ball cap with Scottish motif.
26. One thistle embroidered hanky.
27. One Buchan blue pottery tankard with a piece of tartan cloth with two small metal crosses attached.
28. One length of tartan ribbon.

PUBLIC COMMENT BOX - ITEMS
SCROLLS
1. One paper – 'Alba My Homeland'.
2. One paper – tied with a ribbon.
3. Two white and lilac papers tied with ribbons.

SEALED ENVELOPES
Numbered 7

VARIOUS
1. One small grey ring box sealed and marked 'Freedom'.
2. Eight thistle-shaped wedding cake favours.
3. Small gauze bag containing lavender.
4. A4 open envelope containing stitch work 'Freedom is Best'.
5. A4 laminated poem by Ian Logan.
6. A4 laminated poem – 'Freedom' by Calum Robertson.
7. A4 poem – 'Independence at Home' by Bill Mejury.
8. Five paper sheets – brass rubbing of the Seal of Stirling.

'MY THOUGHTS ON WILLIAM WALLACE' – SMITH QUESTIONNAIRE.
i) White - 14
ii) Blue – 70 (including one attached to a small Saltire).
iii) Yellow – 36
iv) Lilac – 30

NOTES
Numbered 12.

DISPLAY CABINET (CONTENTS)
1. One flag – the Saltire.
2. Small piece of plaid tied with a yellow metal chain.
3. One small dark blue teddy bear with embroidered Saltire on chest.
4. One small navy blue box tied with a blue ribbon.

5. Small bottle of Johnnie Walker whisky.
6. Paper scroll with green Celtic border tied with gold-coloured ribbon and a sprig of heather.
7. One note addressed to Sir William Wallace, Guardian of Scotland.
8. One yellow envelope addressed 'Tales o' the Wallace' by Allandale.
9. Dried thistle on a card addressed to Sir William Wallace.
10. Box lid showing a dried thistle and Saltire made by S Lynn.
11. Small piece of mica with sprig of white silk flowers in cotton tied with ribbon to hold message on paper.
12. Glass fridge magnet showing a portrait of Sir William Wallace.
13. Badge with the words 'Pro Liberate' inscribed.
14. Small piece of cotton cloth embroidered with the words 'Honour and Freedom'.
15. Small piece of cloth embroidered with a thistle with thistle brooch attached signed BRH, Alison Lowrie, Stirling.
16. Sprig from the thorn tree in the grounds of Dumfermline Abbey attached to a note advising of its significance. Signed by Carnock family, Dumfermline.

WREATH CARDS
i) Wallace Heritage Trust.
ii) Braidfoot Familly, Texas, USA.
iii) The Chivalric Order of the Temple of Jerusalem, The Scottish Knights Templar.

Service of Commemoration

for

Sir William Wallace

The Priory Church of
St. Bartholomew the Great
London

23 August 2005 at 3.00pm

Officiating Minister
Rev. Alan Sorensen
BD, MTh, Dip.Min, FSA(Scot)

Organist
Christopher Whitton
BA (Cantab), MMus, FRCO

Hymn

**Behold! The Mountain
Of The Lord**
Tune: GLASGOW

Behold! the mountain of the Lord
in latter days shall rise
On mountain tops above the hills,
and draw the wondering eyes.

Among the nations he shall judge;
his judgments truth shall guide;
His sceptre shall protect the just,
and quell the sinner's pride.

No strife shall rage, nor hostile feuds
disturb those peaceful years;
To ploughshares men shall beat their sword
to pruning-hooks their spears.

No longer hosts, encountering hosts
shall crowds of slain deplore:
They hang the trumpet in the hall,
and study war no more.

*Scottish Paraphrases, 1781
from Isaiah 2.2-5*

Benediction

Recessional

"Lord Lovat's Lament"
Piper: Lt. Cmdr. James Gee

*The congregation is asked to remain
standing until the casket is carried from
the church.*

Welcome

Call to prayer
Prayer

Wallace: A Man For All Seasons?
Dr. Fiona Watson PhD

"I'm Coming Home"
Ted Christopher

Scripture Readings

Old Testament
Psalm 22:1-18

Epistle
Ephesians 6:10-20

Reflection on Wallace
Alex. Salmond MP

"Flower of Scotland"
Ronnie Brown

Reflection on Wallace
David R. Ross

Hymn

For The Healing Of The Nations
Tune: CWM RHONDDA
(nb - the last line of each verse is repeated)

For the healing of the nations,
Lord we pray with one accord.
For a just and equal sharing
of the things that earth affords.
To a life of love in action,
help us rise and pledge our word.

Lead us, Father, into freedom,
from despair your world release;
That, redeemed from war and hatred,
men may come and go in peace.
Show us how through care and goodness
fear will die and hope increase.

All that kills abundant living,
let it from the earth be banned;
Pride of status, race or schooling,
dogmas keeping man from man.
In our common quest for justice,
may we hallow life's brief span.

You, Creator God, have written
your great name on all mankind;
For our growing in your likeness,
bring the life of Christ to mind;
That by our response and service
earth its destiny may find.

Fred Kaan

Scripture Reading

Gospel

Homily

Act of Remembrance

During this, members of the congregation are invited to come forward and place their cards within the casket.

As we do so
Coisir Lunnainn
will sing:

"Psalm 65"
Tune: French

"Caol Muile"
(Iona Boat Song)

This commemorates dead kings of Scotland being rowed to their final resting place on the Isle of Iona.

"Tuireadh Iain Ruaidh"
(Lament for Red Iain)

A lament for a husband and a great hero, Red Haired Iain, lost on the field of battle.

"An Innis Aigh"
(The Beloved Isle)

An exile thinking of death and his final resting place with his beloved – the Beloved Isle – a metaphor for Heaven.

The congregation is asked to stand as the casket is piped into the church.

Introit

"The Flowers of the Forest"
Piper: Lt. Cmdr. James Gee

"Scots Wha Hae"
Soloist: Ian McAllister

Hymn

Here Hangs a Man Discarded
Tune PASSION CHORALE

Here hangs a man discarded,
a scarecrow hoisted high,
A nonsense pointing nowhere
to all who hurry by.
Can such a clown of sorrows
still bring a useful word
Where faith and love seem phantoms
and every hope absurd?

Yet here is help and comfort
to lives by comfort bound,
When drums of dazzling progress
give strangely hollow sound:
Life emptied of all meaning,
drained out in bleak distress,
Can share in broken silence
our deepest emptiness;

And love that freely entered
the pit of life's despair
Can name our hidden darkness
and suffer with us there.
Lord, if you now are risen,
help all who long for light
To hold the hand of promise
till faith receives its sight.

Brian Wren

155

Some other books published by **LUATH** Press

A Passion for Scotland
David R Ross
ISBN 1 84282 019 2
PBK £5.99

David R Ross is passionate about Scotland's past. And its future. In this heartfelt journey through Scotland's story he shares his passion for what it means to be a Scot.

Eschewing xenophobia, his deep understanding of how Scotland's history touches her people shines through. All over Scotland, into England and Europe, over to Canada, Chicago and Washington – the people and places that bring Scotland's story to life, and death. Includes:

The Early Scots
Wallace and Bruce
The Union
Montrose
The Jacobites
John Maclean
Tartan Day USA

And, revealed for the first time: the burial places of all Scotland's monarchs.

Desire Lines: A Scottish Odyssey
David R Ross
ISBN 1 84282 033 8
PBK £9.99

A must read for every Scot, everyone living in Scotland and everyone visiting Scotland!

David R Ross not only shows us his Scotland but he teaches us it too. You feel as though you are on the back of his motorcycle listening to the stories of his land as you fly with him up and down the smaller roads, the 'desire lines', of Scotland. Ross takes us off the beaten track and away from the main routes chosen for us by modern road builders.

He starts our journey in England and criss-crosses the border telling the bloody tales of the towns and villages. His recounting of Scottish history, its myths and its legends is unapologetically and unashamedly pro-Scots.

Pride and passion for his country, the people, the future of Scotland; and his uncompromising patriotism shines through *Desire Lines*, David R Ross's homage to his beloved country.

David Ross is a passionate patriot. He is not afraid of stating his opinion, and he does so with unabashed gusto.
JANE ROBINSON, SCOTS MAGAZINE

On the Trail of
William Wallace
David R Ross
ISBN 0 946487 47 2
PBK £7.99

On the Trail of Robert
the Bruce
David R Ross
ISBN 0 946487 52 9
PBK £7.99

On the Trail of William Wallace offers a refreshing insight into the life and heritage of the great Scots hero who whose proud story is at the very heart of what it means to be Scottish. Not concentrating simply on the hard historical facts of Wallace's life, the book also takes into account the real significance of Wallace and his effect on the ordinary Scot through the ages, manifested in the many sites where his memory is marked.

In trying to piece together the jigsaw of the reality of Wallace's life David Ross weaves a subtle flow of new information with his own observations. His engaging, thoughtful and at times amusing narrative reads with the ease of a historical novel, complete with all the intrigue, treachery and romance required to hold the attention of the casual reader and still entice the more knowledgeable historian.

...an impressive collection of local folklore and little-known fact alongside the story of Wallace's life, offering an off-beat tourist trail for the historically minded.
SCOTLAND ON SUNDAY

On the Trail of Robert the Bruce charts the story of Scotland's hero-king from his boyhood, through his days of indecision as Scotland suffered under the English yoke, to his assumption of the crown, six months after the death of William Wallace.

Here is the astonishing blow by blow account of how, against fearful odds, Bruce lead the Scots to win their greatest ever victory. Bannockburn was not the end of the story. The war against English oppression lasted another fourteen years. Bruce lived just long enough to see his dreams of an independent Scotland come to fruition in 1328 with the signing of the Treaty of Edinburgh. The trail takes us to Bruce's sites in Scotland, many of the little known and forgotten battle sites of northern England, and as far afield as the Bruce monuments in Andalusia and Jerusalem.

David R. Ross is a proud patriot and an unashamed romantic.
SCOTLAND ON SUNDAY

Braveheart: From Hollywood to Holyrood
Lin Anderson
ISBN 1 84282 066 4
PBK £7.99

Braveheart was the best film of 1995, winning five Oscars and re-establishing the historical epic as a film genre, paving the way for the successes of *Gladiator* and *Lord of the Rings* that followed.

Braveheart reached a global audience with its powerful re-telling of the almost forgotten story of William Wallace and his struggle to defend Scotland's freedom. Described as 'the most politically influential movie of the 20th century' it also had a part to play in the political change that swept Scotland, mobilising public opinion to aid the return of Scottish Parliament after a gap of 300 years.

Braveheart: From Hollywood to Holyrood is the first book about this movie phenomenon, discussing the life and legacy of William Wallace through the modern image of the hero as presented in the film. Written with the co-operation of Randall Wallace, author of the screenplay and novelisation of Braveheart and including never before published photographs, this is the long-awaited handbook for Braveheart fans around the world.

Those in whose veins the love of free-dom and/or Mel Gibson runs will thrill to the vox pop plaudits here from cin-emagoers worldwide.
THE SCOTSMAN

The Wallace Muse: poems & artwork inspired by the life & legend of William Wallace
ed. Lesley Duncan & Elspeth King
ISBN 1 905222 29 7
PBK £7.99

The power of Wallace
Cuts through art
But art calls attention to it
Badly or well
from 'Lines for Wallace' by Edwin Morgan

Sir William Wallace – bloodthirsty and battle-hardened hero, liberator and cre-ator of Scotland. Wallace the man was a complex character – loved by the Scots, loathed by the English, a terror to some, an inspirational leader to others. No mat-ter what side you are on, William Wallace is an unmistakable and unforgettable his-torical figure.

The life and legend of Wallace has been a Muse providing inspiration to poets and artists from Scotland and across the globe for 700 years. From great epic to McGonagall, the violent to the poignant, this collection highlights the impact that the memory of Wallace has made on the nation's culture for centuries.

The highlight is undoubtedly Morgan's passionate new poem which has been praised by critics as a 'remarkable' work which 'gets straight to the heart' of the matter.
THE TIMES

Blind Harry's Wallace

William Hamilton of
Gilbertfield
Introduced by Elspeth King
ISBN 0 946487 33 2
PBK £8.99

The original story of the real brave-heart, Sir William Wallace.

Racy, blood on every page, violently anglophobic, grossly embellished, vulgar and disgusting, clumsy and stilted, a literary failure, a great epic. Whatever the verdict on BLIND HARRY, this is the book which has done more than any other to frame the notion of Scotland's national identity. Despite its numerous 'historical inaccuracies', it remains the principal source for what we now know about the life of Wallace.

The novel and film *Braveheart* were based on the 1722 Hamilton edition of this epic poem. Burns, Wordsworth, Byron and others were greatly influenced by this version 'wherein the old obsolete words are rendered more intelligible', which is said to be the book, next to the Bible, most commonly found in Scottish households in the eighteenth century. Burns even admits to having 'borrowed... a couplet worthy of Homer' directly from Hamilton's version of BLIND HARRY to include in 'Scots wha hae'.

The story of Wallace poured a Scottish prejudice in my veins which will boil along until the floodgates of life shut in eternal rest.
ROBERT BURNS

Over the Top with the Tartan Army

Andrew McArthur
ISBN 0 946487 45 6
PBK £7.99

Thankfully, the days of the draft and character-building National Service are no more. In their place, Scotland has witnessed the growth of a new and curious military phenomenon. Grown men bedecked in tartan, yomping across most of the globe, hellbent on benevolence and ritualistic bevvying. Often chanting a profane mantra about a popular football pundit. In what noble cause do they serve? Why football, of course – at least, in theory.

Following the ailing fortunes of Scotland isn't easy. But the famous Tartan Army has broken the pain barrier on numerous occasions, emerging as cultural ambassadors for Scotland. Their total dedication to debauchery has spawned stories and legends that could have evaporated in a drunken haze but for the memory of one hardy footsoldier: Andrew McArthur.

'Over the Top' is a labour of love – a bit like following Scotland, if truth be told. This book is a must for any football fan who likes a good laugh. Because if you love Scottish football you've got to have a sense of humour.

I commend this book to all football supporters... You are left once more feeling slightly proud that these stupid creatures are your own countrymen.
GRAHAM SPIERS, SCOTLAND ON SUNDAY

Luath Press Limited
committed to publishing well written books worth reading

LUATH PRESS takes its name from Robert Burns, whose little collie Luath (*Gael.*, swift or nimble) tripped up Jean Armour at a wedding and gave him the chance to speak to the woman who was to be his wife and the abiding love of his life. Burns called one of The Twa Dogs Luath after Cuchullin's hunting dog in Ossian's *Fingal*. Luath Press was established in 1981 in the heart of Burns country, and is now based a few steps up the road from Burns' first lodgings on Edinburgh's Royal Mile. Luath offers you distinctive writing with a hint of unexpected pleasures. Most bookshops in the UK, the US, Canada, Australia, New Zealand and parts of Europe, either carry our books in stock or can order them for you. To order direct from us, please send a £sterling cheque, postal order, international money order or your credit card details (number, address of cardholder and expiry date) to us at the address below. Please add post and packing as follows: UK – £1.00 per delivery address; overseas surface mail – £2.50 per delivery address; overseas airmail – £3.50 for the first book to each delivery address, plus £1.00 for each additional book by airmail to the same address. If your order is a gift, we will happily enclose your card or message at no extra charge.

Luath Press Limited
543/2 Castlehill
The Royal Mile
Edinburgh
EH1 2ND
Scotland

Telephone: 0131 225 4326 (24 hours)
Fax: 0131 225 4324
email: sales@luath.co.uk
Website: www.luath.co.uk